The Smart Seeker's Guide to

Spiritual Bullshit

Sue Fitzmaurice

REBEL
MAGIC

REBEL
MAGIC

To all the friends who've helped me shovel my shit.

Also by Sue Fitzmaurice

Fiction

Angels in the Architecture

Non-fiction

Purpose – the Elements of Purpose

Purpose 2 – Making Sure your Purpose finds You

The Accidental Mary Pilgrimage

Billow & Breeze – A Journey through the Scottish Islands

The Deliberate Mary Pilgrimage

Journeys with the Divine Feminine (ed)

You seek too much information and not enough transformation.

~ *Sai Baba*

The first half of life is devoted to forming a healthy ego,
the second half is going inward and letting go of it.

~ *CG Jung*

Life is simple. Everything happens for you, not to you. Everything
happens at exactly the right moment, neither too soon or too late.
You don't have to like it, it's just easier if you do.

~ *Byron Katie*

If you're stuck up your own arse, all you'll see is shit.

~ *Sue Fitzmaurice*

Where are you? Here.
What time is it? Now.
What are you? This moment.

~ *Dan Millman*

The transformation of the heart is a wondrous thing,
no matter how you land there.

~*Patti Smith*

Note to the Reader

I use New Zealand English, which is more or less the same as UK English. Those unused to this may stumble over the *u* of neighbour and the verb of *practise*. There is no word *gotten* in the Queen's English and we *minimise* without a *z* (which we pronounce *zed*). Quotations from others are in the version of English of their nationality or first publication. Any other errors are mine.

Contents

Introduction

Religion and spiritual pursuits have been a part of my life since I was very young. My parents were Anglican, which is derived from the Church of England. My brother and I went to Sunday School and were confirmed in the Anglican Church of *All Saints* in Palmerston North, New Zealand, where we grew up. We both served at the altar and my brother set up the first youth group there. He went on to join the Baptist Church, later completing a Bachelor of Divinities and becoming a pastor. That career path came to a halt after he and his wife experienced almost soul-destroying bullying, although they remained members of the Church. I briefly engaged with fundamentalism as a teenager, but I was disillusioned with aspects of it. When I saw a young, single mother with a baby put a hundred dollars in the collection bag one Sunday, a line was drawn in my mind and soul about what was okay about religion and what wasn't. During this same period, our mother became ill and died. I was twenty and it turned my world upside-down overnight. She'd been at the centre of my universe and I had to understand why she'd gone and where she was. I pursued religious and philosophical thought with a vigour. It was the mid-80s and in my small town that meant going to the public library, which didn't have a whole lot to say on the topic. One line in the conclusion of a small book about the world's major religions was enough. It said that the Baha'i Faith combined elements of all of the world's religions into its philosophy. I'd already reached a point of understanding that truth and light existed in all of the world's faiths, but I couldn't accept their exclusivity. It made no sense to me that any religion could proclaim itself the only way to God. I believed they were all a part of the same divine plan. I eagerly sought out the Baha'i Faith, reading about it voraciously, and I met and talked with the local Baha'is – a bunch of very normal, sometimes hippyish, generally professional and educated people. I was reluctant to join an organised religion but ultimately it spoke truth to me and I made that commitment and remained an active Baha'i for over twenty years. A few years after becoming a Baha'i, I immersed myself also in the world of *Transcendental Meditation,* discovering the science of consciousness, a wonderful companion to my religion that remains a part of my life today. By my early forties though, I found myself dissatisfied. It was hard to find a book anymore that truly moved me. I felt stuck. A series of circumstances led me to an introduction to *Qi gong* and energy healing, and through these and other modalities I began a new exploration of the universe and my relationship with it. I left the Baha'i Faith soon after, not because I no longer believed or accepted it, but because I felt restricted once again by the walls of religion. Whilst the Baha'i Faith is one that encourages questions and exploration, there are only so many hours in a day and I knew I had to spend them elsewhere.

I'm not and never have been someone who criticises religion for its faults, albeit that I have often been quick to criticise the followers, and particularly the leadership, of religions, for their narrow-mindedness and judgement of others. All religions have rules and where they invoke fear at disobedience is where I part company with them. Religion does, however, teach discipline, and where it's doing its job properly it provides an opportunity for depth of exploration. These and many other great spiritual benefits make most religions of incredible value to their adherents and to society as a whole.

My spiritual exploration and education have been broad and taken me via many disciplines, teachings, religions, experiences, countries, people, politics, practices, and worship. Every one of these has provided valued lessons and growth. Oftentimes that growth has come with pain – I've almost always been grateful for it, at least in hindsight.

But in every instance also I have come up against the arrogant, the judgemental, the cruel, the needy, the irresponsible, the jealous, the condescending, the self-righteous, the humourless, the attention-seeking, the angry, the idiotic, the miserable, the loud, the over-politically correct, and the ignorant. And I have been one of them.

For many people, spirituality is a bandwagon. It involves doing certain things that are seen outwardly as expressions of spirituality – dressing a certain way, being vegan, going to yoga classes – but that ignore the deeper and truer aspects of genuine spiritual inquiry and contemplation. Spirituality becomes a way to feel superior, no different than seeking academic achievement or career advancement.

In the pursuit of the spiritual, there is nothing so true as *a little bit of knowledge is a dangerous thing.* There is no other arena where so many experts exist who know so little but are so very willing to proclaim it. There is both massive diversity and thunderous NOISE in the spiritual world – the diversity is brilliant – the noise not so much. This is about some of the noise – the kinds of things a lot of people do and say that cloak them in judgement, arrogance and stupidity, often leaving others hurt.

This book is meant to be both humorous and serious. You will no doubt recognise much of what is said, hopefully in yourself as much as in others. It is in the extent to which we recognise our own arrogance and ignorance that we find opportunities to take further steps into real truth along the spiritual highway.

Most of what is written here has at least two sides to it. Because ultimately there is a bit of truth – or a lot – in everything. I love the contradictions entailed in believing the universe brings us everything, at the same time being able to poke a stick at the nonsense of that. I believe in the power of the universe, but I'm a bit over it being used as an excuse for everything that goes right or wrong in our lives. I believe in prayers and healing but I'm a bit over being asked to send them every five minutes for every big or small piece of crap going on in the world or in someone's life. I get that things others do or say can trigger reactions in us but I'm a bit over those reactions manifesting into crappy behaviour, especially where it's aimed at other people and masks the responsibility one has to deal with one's own shit. I love that so many people are experiencing a spiritual awakening in the world, but I'm a bit over seeing it used as a club with which to beat one's loved ones and others.

I'm not interested here in examining beliefs in whatever religion or philosophy or tradition you may follow; whether Mary Magdalene was Jesus' consort, whether past lives exist, or whether God exists in all of nature. These and thousands of other beliefs and understandings are for your own personal examination and discovery. (Although, please, for heaven's sake, neither Celts nor Druids built the stone circles.) I'm interested in the things we do and say in the name of our beliefs that are used as weapons of judgement and excuses for bad behaviour, of which there are many more than I mention here.

The world is suffering a massive polarisation presently, not so much of beliefs, but of people's expression of their beliefs. Beliefs are held to with a vehemence that serves to isolate and divide rather than unite and strengthen. The reality is that there are over seven billion different spiritual perspectives in the world and not one of them is the only right one. As to the expression of those beliefs, if it rests on a foundation of love for all, then it's fine by me. If it is used to justify a single act of unkindness then there is work to be done on it, and that is in truth the case for all of us to some extent or another.

Writing this has caused me to examine much of my own beliefs and behaviour, so much so that at times I've twisted myself up in knots trying to say what I mean. Words are a part of my journey. They can be profound and life-giving; they can be nit-picking, stupid and hurtful; and yet other times they, like we, need to get over themselves and not be taken so seriously. Ultimately, it's about committing to *continuing*, because there is no end-point in this progress of one's soul. It's wonderful to have those beautiful spiritual experiences hopefully we've all had – moments of insight and elation – but the real nitty-gritty of this work is always going to be about fronting up. Fronting up to your own baloney, owning it, figuring it out, dealing with it, moving on. That's the real work of spirituality and if you think it's not then you're kidding yourself.

Most recently – and rather surprisingly to me – my own journey has brought me back to the Church; not as a Christian (although I don't disbelieve in the mission of Jesus), but in the discovery of the magic and beauty of the women saints, most particularly the Marys – the Mother and the Magdalene. It's been enlightening, joyful, deeply moving, and on occasion incredibly sad.

Simultaneously though, very large amounts of excrement descended upon me. When you dive into a clear stream, you always stir up the silt on the bottom. You cannot have exquisite spiritual flow without sometimes finding a kink in your hose. It can be very easy to blame someone else for standing on it, but there is almost always some work for you yourself to do, regardless of what others may be saying or doing to you. And if you're the one standing on someone else's hose – which has been all of us too – then get the hell off and play nice!

This book is a mass of irony and contradiction and I hope all the better for it. You'll want to disagree with me. Go for it! You'll spot inconsistencies and discrepancies. That's kind of the point. Or one of them. Having perspective doesn't just mean standing back – it means standing back and seeing there are *multiple* ways of looking at something. We ignore that multiplicity at our spiritual peril.

Please be clear that this is not a book with which to beat up others. Or yourself, for that matter. People's truth is their own. If it provides some insight into your interaction with others, great. Better though that it's a tool, however humble, for your own consideration and development.

Finally, if I had to say what my own beliefs are now, after so much exploration, it would be simply that we are here to learn to love ourselves and others better; and therein lies an infinite journey of humility and growth.

It's not important if you agree or disagree with me.
After all, most of what I'm giving you is really theory.
And no theory adequately covers reality. I'm speaking to you,
not of the truth, but of obstacles to it.
I cannot describe the truth. No one can.
All I can do is give you a description of your falsehoods,
so that you can drop them.
All I can do for you is help you unlearn.
That's what spirituality is all about: unlearning,
unlearning almost everything you've been taught.
A willingness to unlearn and to listen.

Anthony de Mello

Bullshit People Say

People spout a lot of bullshit. We're surrounded by it every day in every aspect of our lives and it's exhausting. There's no area of our lives where this is more prevalent than in politics and religion. Whilst there are equally vast bastions of truth and authenticity to be found here, the extent to which these two aspects of our daily lives blast us with utter bollocks is frightening. Within spirituality, there are some particular lines that are trotted out regularly that although often meant well, can blind the practitioner to a more useful truth. Others can be downright damaging. A grieving friend mentioned to me recently that *God wanted them back* was the one line that really made her want to poke the eyes out of the person who uttered it. I can imagine.

The problem with a lot of spiritual truths is that some are actually true – on one particular level. On another level, they may be false, or they may need to be tempered with other truths. *Gospel* is a word that strictly speaking refers to the four gospels of the Bible, the gospels of the Saints: Matthew, Mark, Luke and John. *Gospel* has also become a colloquialism for truth – we might tell someone that something's *the gospel truth,* not meaning it in any way to have anything to do with the Bible or Christianity. The actual Gospels might not be viewed as truth in any non-relative sense even by many Christians, who would rightly view much of the Bible as metaphor and allegory – a basis for a consideration of what *could* be *a* truth, and relative to where one's spiritual development and understanding are at.

Truth therefore is relative. It has always been relative and it always will be. *Fact* is another matter. Don't entangle the two.

> The opposite of a correct statement is a false statement.
> But the opposite of a profound truth
> may well be another profound truth.
>
> *Niels Bohr*

At some point, figuring out what's truth and what's not, can have you turning mental somersaults. To some extent, this book is going to add to that, although I hope equally it will assist in dispensing with some of those gymnastics too. There's a lot about our spiritual journey and understanding that can do our heads in – like much of our life, it's a process of eliminating what we *don't* want in order to see what we *do*. It's about deciding how we *don't* want to live, in order to see how we *do*. It's about the long and hazardous road of separating bullshit from not-bullshit, and slipping in it occasionally, if not often. And then understanding that rather than eliminating the bullshit, we can see it all as useful compost for our own growth. Nothing is wasted.

'*Just let it go*'

There are a lot of stupid lines people come out with – *forget it and move on* is a particularly annoying one, and in a similar vein: *just let it go*. Not only are these very often impossible to achieve (which will only add to any sense of failure one might already have), but it can be very damaging to bury something without working through causes and effects and learning from the painful things that happen to us. There is no value in running away from pain and there is much to be learned from sitting with it and figuring it out.

Grief takes the time it takes and there is no appropriate length of time one should be 'allowed' to grieve, nor can one person's grief by definition be especially more or less than some other person's – size isn't an issue here.

There is nothing harder than letting go of something you've become attached to, and there's nothing worse than not only someone suggesting you do so, but suggesting you *just* need to do it – as though it's like dropping something hot from your hand. Letting go of other people and addictions is the hardest of all. Anyone who tells you to *just* let go isn't helping you.

You may well need to let go of many things, but you will rarely *just* do it. It's a process; it takes time and there can be many steps along the way. Cold turkey can work for some things, but even then, you'll generally go through hell for a time – as may those around you.

Letting go too quickly can also mean you might miss valuable learning opportunities. The notion that everything happens for a reason has some value – it's not the be all and end all, but it's always worth a look.

We're generally powerless to let go until something in us shifts enough that whatever has been causing our suffering lets go of us, not the other way around. When there is nothing more to learn, then our attraction to our suffering de-magnetises and we detach. Like many spiritual truths, *letting go* is something that we can understand on different levels – at one point knowing we can't let it go until it lets go of us, and on another level, knowing we must let go just the same. If you can find your way through that contradiction, you'll go far.

Almost always, our attachment will reflect back to us something about our own self that we need to look at. Probably not something we really *want* to look at either. That's just the way it is. It's hanging on because you haven't learned what you're supposed to yet.

Don't beat yourself up for not having let go of some things. It's fine. It'll take the time it takes.

'Thoughts and prayers'

A mother of a victim in a recent American mass shooting said: *I don't want prayers. I don't want thoughts. I want gun control. I hope to God nobody else sends me any more prayers.*

I find this compelling. Add to that what I've no doubt is the reality: that most people who say they're sending *thoughts and prayers* actually aren't.

Do you really believe all those politicians who say in their speeches that something-or-other, or someone-or-other, is in their thoughts and prayers? I don't. And I don't think I'm just being cynical.

Recently there was a worldwide prayer vigil for rain in Australia in the context of the country's horrific bush fires. Just the one prayer vigil. Coincidentally there was a little rain fell a day later in one small part of the country, and success was claimed by the prayerful. It does actually rain in Australia. Often, even. Considering the success claimed, one might imagine there'd be additional worldwide prayer vigils, but even the horrors of Australia's burning eventually exited the news cycle, and so too did this particular urge to help. But maybe the prayers did help.

When it comes to people I know personally, I'm kind of up for sending positive energy your way if you're in a bind, but I'll probably not spend more than a few seconds or a few minutes doing so, and since I'm not an energy magician I doubt very much that I will make any difference to your circumstances. What I *will* do, is give you concrete help if it's within my power to do so. So if you've got a job interview coming up, I reckon I can make a ton of difference helping you prepare for it. It's something I'm good at. If you're in a financial bind, I might have twenty quid to spare, or more. If there's shit going down in your life, then I'll happily get online and chat with you for however long you need to vent, and maybe I'll find a way to give you some self-care advice without sounding patronising. But *thoughts and prayers?* Nup.

Now, I do know people who *are* very good at sending positive energy, and I believe we can all learn to be transmitters of positive energy too. But that's not what most people are doing when they say they're sending *thoughts and prayers.* And if you're someone who's constantly asking for people to send *thoughts and prayers,* you may need to be learning how to create more positive outcomes in your life for yourself.

At the very least, please don't tell victims of mass gun violence – or people who've lost everything in the Armageddon of Australia's fires – that you're sending *thoughts and prayers* if you're not also going to take action against gun violence and climate change, because it's bullshit.

'You create your own reality'

The problem with this truth is in the way it's portrayed, and for those wanting to develop themselves personally, this can create a sense of guilt and uselessness that is hard to move beyond.

The law of attraction is frequently misunderstood. It seems like a great idea that you can simply think differently and hey presto everything will be perfect. Not only is this simplistic, it's also dangerous. Few of us can change our thoughts that easily for a start, and immediately we fail to do so – which will be often – we'll beat ourselves up for our failure.

The other danger of an amateur approach to the law of attraction is thinking of it in terms of right and wrong, or good and bad, thinking. We confuse it with the laws of karma and wonder what we must have done wrong in order to have attracted some particular piece of bullshit in our lives. This leads to blaming ourselves for everything that happens to us, which isn't useful. Many of us are already overloaded with guilt, blame and shame, and it's too easy to add to it.

That we create our own reality is an early discovery for most of us on our spiritual journeys. And as with many other spiritual truths, we tend to skim the surface of knowledge on this very important topic, when we should be going deeper and really coming to grips with its intricacies and the deeper levels of its meaning. No spiritual truth, properly understood, should make us feel bad about ourselves – if it does, it's either not a spiritual truth or you've only examined it at a surface level. Go deeper.

'She's an old soul'

Truth: Every soul is as old as every other soul. All souls left Source at the same time.

Truth: *If* there were a truth that some souls are older than other souls, that doesn't make the 'old soul' somehow better than any other. If you've spent a hundred lives on this planet being a bitch, and I've spent one being an angel, you're not fucking better than me!

Truth: A precocious child is not necessarily an old soul. A very sweet child is not necessarily an old soul. Even if there were a truth that some souls are older than other souls, *nobody actually knows how old your soul is.*

Truth: Even if there were a truth that some souls are older than other souls, *it doesn't mean anything.*

The idea of *old souls* is pure ego and a way that a lot of people who consider themselves spiritual put themselves above others. You might as well be a nasty old priest in the Middle Ages looking down on your illiterate flock. If you need to put yourself above others, you have a spiritual problem.

Just because you are pursuing the spiritual and others aren't – or at least not obviously to you – doesn't make you better, wiser, smarter, or deeper.

Talk of *old souls* needs to stop in the spiritual community. It's an arrogance and a very damaging one. Even if it has truth – and I don't believe it does – and even if you are an old soul, nothing about that makes your journey in this life any easier or any better. You've just found another BMW for your spiritual garage – you may think it makes you look good, but you still have to wipe your arse every day like everyone else. And meanwhile, a lot of other people will think: *there goes another BMW driver/spiritual wanker.* Don't be a spiritual wanker.

'Listen to your gut'

This is an increasingly common social media meme lately. *'If it feels wrong, it probably is.'* That kind of thing. You will have seen several different versions of this notion.

Here's the thing though. Most of us take *years* to discern the difference between, on the one hand, our gut or intuition, and on the other hand, some fear peculiar to us that's been triggered. Your 'gut' is generally not telling you that someone's energy is wrong for you – that's usually a reaction you're having to your buttons being pushed.

When we give into our fears in this way, we're missing the opportunity to look at our own shit in favour of looking at what we think is someone else's. The other person will have some shit, because all of us always do, but your job is to examine your own, not theirs. Other people's 'stuff' should not be used as an excuse for us to not look at our own.

Sometimes your gut *is* telling you to avoid a certain person, but we all need to develop our skills in this regard. Here's the thing: if you're on a first date with someone and your gut is saying this one's not for you, your gut is probably right. If you're having a coffee out with a friend you've known for years and your 'gut' is telling you this person is wrong for you, that's probably *not* your gut – it's probably some fear of your own that you need to take a look at.

If you're not sure, then find the time to get firmly into your heart and soul – as opposed to your ego – and ask the question. Nine times out of ten, it's your ego doing its job and sending warning signals that prevent you from examining yourself.

'Be positive'

Especially annoying when said by someone with dreadlocks and John Lennon sunglasses, who carries a tin whistle, and has a name like Shaolin Rama or Isis Rhiannon.

Emphasising positivity can be a great way of ignoring important emotional issues, not to mention a great deal of shit that's happening in the world generally.

There's massive value in gratitude, and indeed in positivity, but it shouldn't be forced at the expense of examining the reality of one's emotions and situation.

It's a difficult challenge to ignore: social media is brimming with memes exhorting us to think positively, and there is absolutely an important learning to be had in changing some of the ways we think and getting our mind out of the negative stories we're addicted to, that keep rolling round and round in our heads. But the 'negative' stuff doesn't just go away because we're not thinking about it, and it may make things worse by ignoring it.

A lot of people in the spiritual community believe that the best thing we can do for the world and all its problems is to not give it any attention, not think about it or talk about it at all – that by talking about it, according to the law of attraction, we continue to create it. There is some truth to this. But while we're busy being positive and ignoring the harsh realities of poverty and the rape culture, other people are making a positive difference in the lives of those suffering at the harsh end of those things. And I'm sure they're being very positive about it. Plus, we all need to vote. And we need to vote in full awareness of the crap in the world and with a view to electing representatives of integrity who will make their best 'positive' efforts to fix things.

> Don't become the person who acquires awareness,
> only to throw it back in someone else's face,
> that it's them who is being negative and not you.
>
> *Tina Addorisio*

Real growth happens in the darkness, and to the extent that the 'be positive' vibe has overtaken us in our spiritual pursuits, it creates a reaction in us to our own darkness(es) that makes us feel like we're way off track when we're struggling against that darkness. Don't struggle against it. Let it in and get into it. Our first response to our darkness is always *I don't want to feel like this* –

this is shit – I hate this – I'm doing it all wrong – I'm no good at life and so on. Pathological positivity is the worst thing you can do. Surrender to the wisdom of your darkness. There isn't a right or a wrong way to navigate your own path – it's *your* path and only you can determine the way to walk it. Everyone's path contains potholes, ruts and crevices that you have to find your way through, around and over. None of us can magically appear on the other side of those bumps and holes – some we can go around, but many we have to go through. They're not an aberration or a mistake – they're a part of our life.

Relentless insistence within the spiritual community on *just raise your vibration* or *just manifest what you want* shames the seeker who isn't feeling that way right now. It makes people think everything's their own fault and it ignores the reality of people's pain and the need to express it and be heard. Ultimately it becomes a form of gaslighting, where you make others think they're crazy for not being able to vibrate higher, manifest everything they want, and be positive. It can be a really shitty thing to do to people, especially if they're struggling. Stop with the 'be positive' bullshit.

Instead of turning your back on someone who's struggling, see an opportunity to practise compassion. If their struggle is affecting you, understand that that's about you. Don't be the she-devil that adds to someone's struggle by informing them of their negativity.

'What's meant to be will always find a way'

Bollocks.

This is usually offered as an explanation of the universe's intentions for someone who's wanting or waiting for a particular outcome. *If it's meant to be* demonstrates another superficial reliance on the far greater and more elaborate science of astrology and numerous other concepts.

There are various elements of truth to the notion that some things are 'meant to be' and it's a concept that echoes through many religions and traditions, as well as ancient cultures and myths, and it's rarely described in those contexts in simple terms.

But in many spiritual circles, where we've borrowed bits and pieces of traditions that we like (and left ones that we don't), cobbling together an often ill-informed and shallow belief structure, this is one of many throwaway lines repeated with shameful triteness.

More particularly, it undermines the truth of creating our own reality, which is the single greatest power that we have.

'Without the rain there would be no rainbow'

Oh, fuck off.

This is telling people that in order to be happy, they have to also be miserable. Because that's life. If we were happy all the time, then what? We wouldn't *really* be happy? That's stupid. My life can actually be a rainbow pretty much every day, without having to regularly have rain in order to appreciate it.

This is another hackneyed line generally trotted out at a time when someone's in need of much more than corny tropes.

Stop it.

If someone's having a rough time, don't tell them they *have* to have a rough time in order to have a not-rough time. It's ridiculous and has no basis in reality.

This unoriginal, moth-eaten saying stems – distantly – from the more complex truth of, and necessity for, contrast, but in the mistaken understanding that contrast simply means good and bad, and therefore happy and sad. A deeper exploration reveals the balance of growth and consolidation, and of finding the light in the dark as a necessary part of growth rather than simply seeing the dark.

The reality of balance is the interdependency of the light and the dark, and not the repression of the dark or the mere tolerance of it. We are to reconcile with our sadness and darkness, not simply put up with them.

'You'll meet a tall, dark, handsome stranger'

I'm not a regular customer of psychics, tarot readers and fortune tellers, but I've connected with them from time to time over the years. Several have been friends. Almost without exception, they've told me I'm going to meet the love of my life in the next six to twelve months.

With similar consistency, they've advised me of my impending wealth. Truthfully, I have quite good karma for money and have come into some nice pockets of it from time to time, but that's never lined up with anyone's predictions.

Isn't that what we all want to hear? As well as that our children will do well. And so on.

If your entire being is focused on getting rich, and you like to circulate around a lot of psychics and tarot card readers, then they are all going to tell you that great wealth is just around the corner. But get this: this isn't necessarily because they are fake, or poor psychics; it's simply that the extent of your desire, and the energy that attaches to that, will be what is picked up by most psychics.

Recently, an acquaintance had become so taken with a relationship with an online friend that he believed he would marry her. He'd never met or spoken to this woman who lived in another country. He travelled to that country to meet her, understanding from *several* psychic friends that he was going to marry her. As it turned out, this woman wasn't real, but the fake internet persona of another person who had also not romantically led the man on at all and had very obviously been at pains to express quite the opposite.

We do not see things as they are.
We see things as we are.

(Attributed to Anaïs Nin, but arising from the Talmud)

I'm a great believer in what we can learn psychically. But as such I'm also aware of the many layers of energetic understanding, and my own ability – or inability – to grasp all of the subtleties involved. All of this kind of information should be taken advisedly and in a context of other perspectives and realities.

'Stay away from toxic people'

Referring to people as toxic reminds me of the way some people are referred to as *illegal*. It used to be when I visited the United States, that I'd have to stand in the immigration line for *Aliens*. Was *Visitor* too much to ask for?

There are people in the world whose actions have made them extremely dangerous. Most of us don't meet those people. The problem with referring to people as toxic is that the statement is misused to refer to anyone we don't like, or anyone who causes us even the slightest harm, or – very often – someone who is otherwise a perfectly good and decent person who for some reason manages to evoke an emotional response in us that we can't handle. That response is your responsibility, not the other person's.

But here of course it gets very muddy. Most of us have been hurt. Some of us, a lot. And the greater the extent of our hurt and the less we've dealt with that hurt, the more likely we are to be affected by other people. More than anything else in the world, it is other people that both hurt us and/or remind us of our hurts.

The emotional reaction we have to someone else's presence in our lives, or even just in the room, is a mirror being held up for us to take a closer look at ourselves. I'm not talking about the presence in the room of your violent partner or rapist – I'm talking about the ordinary person you may barely know to whom you're experiencing an emotional reaction. That reaction is yours, not theirs. Deal with it.

> We have to differentiate between our intuition guiding us, and our fears triggering us.
>
> *Sue Fitzmaurice*

Most of us have been on retreats, in workshops, or at work conferences at some time. There are always people you don't get along with, whose energy doesn't gel with yours. And there'll be others who are good energetic fits for us and, given a choice, we'll tend to hang out with those people more than others. Those others though, they're not toxic, they're not bad, they're not anything other than just other people. What I've seen frequently in spiritual workshops is the tendency of many participants – and even hosts – to assess the energy of others present, deciding who is where on their spiritual journey and what is wrong with them. Everyone is in fact where they're at, you don't know where they're at, everyone's path is different, and if you're reacting to the place that you think someone else is at, that's about you, not them.

With a few obvious exceptions, there is no value to us on our spiritual journeys in cotton-wooling ourselves up and avoiding the people in our lives who are more of a challenge – for whatever reason – for us to be with. Your spiritual journey should be taking you in the direction of tolerance of more and more people, not fewer and fewer. (By which I don't mean more numbers of people but more diversity of people.) If you're finding yourself able to handle fewer people rather than more, then your spiritual journey needs a look at, because it's not supposed to work that way.

I do understand that at a certain point we like to create a comfortable space to be in that meets our needs for spiritual nourishment – a quiet place with time alone and space to meditate and the people we like the most around us and so on – but generally the idea that someone's energy isn't right for us should be an indicator of work *we* need to do.

> Everyone is our mirror, and the reflection of things we don't like about ourselves is most vivid in those who have the same qualities. In other words, you may see a piece of yourself in this other person even if you don't realise it.
>
> *Don Miguel Ruiz Jr*

It doesn't matter where people are on some imaginary spectrum of being good or bad for you. When you heal your own heart, and trust yourself, then people can only relate to you in ways that suit you.

'Respect my boundaries'

Happy to. If they're not the usual ones though you'll need to tell me what they are before you expect me to follow them.

Boundaries always used to be something you put in place for your children. It was about guiding them into the kind of person you wanted them to be. Things like not talking back, ensuring both parents were consistent in their parenting, keeping bedrooms tidy, doing homework, using good manners, and adhering to curfew times.

Then boundaries became something we applied to our partner relationships, to ensure we had our own space, that we weren't having to mother our partner, and to make sure we weren't being treated as an unpaid slave.

Now boundaries are everywhere, in every relationship. It's become a catchword to protect yourself against anything you don't want, including what you don't want to have to deal with *that you should be dealing with*.

- Someone pushes your buttons: they're stepping over your boundaries? No. You're not dealing with your own shit.
- Someone asks for your help and you're incapable of saying no: they're not respecting your boundaries? No. You need to feel okay about saying no, and not abruptly either – calmly, respectfully. It's okay for people to ask for help – good on them for learning to ask – it's not always an easy thing.
- If your partner wants a conversation with you about some aspect of your relationship, you don't get to pull out the boundaries excuse in order to not have the conversation. You can use it to determine when and how you have the conversation, but not if. They're your partner. You have a responsibility to listen to each other.

'Boundaries' is becoming an over-used excuse for not facing many things you ought to be dealing with. And like a lot of words that get over-used – and abused – it will start to lose its truly relevant and important meaning.

If you're so fragile that you need a lot of boundaries to be able to cope with the world, then it's your own inner strength and wisdom that need more construction work, not a bunch of walls that push other people away from you. And it's often those closest to us that we're pushing away with the boundary excuse.

> Your boundary need not be an angry electric fence that shocks those who touch it. It can be a consistent light around you that announces: I will be treated sacredly.

Jaiya John

Boundaries are put in place to determine where your responsibility ends and someone else's begins, thus we'll have boundaries about our children completing their chores. But it's not my responsibility to know where your 'no' lies, especially if it may be in a different place from a lot of other people's – it's for you to tell me, because that's your responsibility.

Other people are not responsible for your emotional well-being – that's your job – so if you've been triggered by something someone's said or done then that's not because they don't respect your boundaries, that's because you can't manage your known triggers.

And here's another thing to think about with your boundaries. Have you got so good at saying no, that you've become selfish? People who've been especially compliant in their lives – so-called doormats and yes people – finally learn to say *no* and, as with a lot of things, can't stop saying it. That said, it's a natural law of physics for a pendulum to swing almost the same distance the other way before it can ever come to rest in the middle. Balance doesn't happen in one step – it's a back and forth experiment that takes time.

Boundaries aren't there to make life easier – they're there to make life better. You're not making it better if you're avoiding dealing with your own stuff.

It's easy to blame someone else for not respecting your boundaries. It's harder to acknowledge when something's your own stuff. If *speaking your truth* about your boundaries is a euphemism for being an arsehole, expect to eventually be called out on your bullshit.

'I'm an empath'

This one's going to get me in a lot of trouble, but here goes.

Empath, as a word, first came into our modern lexicon in the late 1980s with the television show *Star Trek: The Next Generation*, when the wonderful Captain Jean-Luc Picard employed the lovely Deanna Troi as ship's counsellor. She was half human and half Betazoid, a telepathic race with the ability to sense emotions.

An empath, therefore, is an invention of science fiction; a person with extra-sensory – superpower – empathy. Just as *The Hulk, Spiderman, Wolverine,* and *Ironman* are fictional characters with their own particular superpowers.

It is not, and never has been, a term that exists in modern psychology. What is used in modern psychology is *highly sensitive person,* so well documented that it has an accepted acronym, HSP.

But let's look at what's meant by *empath* in the spiritual community.

There are two main definitions and they variously overlap according to who's describing it – it's very imprecise within spiritual circles. One is that empaths *feel* a whole lot more than they think; the other is that empaths can feel what *you're* feeling, and that that's unavoidable for them. In both instances these can be viewed as special traits to be admired.

In the first instance, not unlike an introvert (in fact very like an introvert), empaths are, among other things, sensitive to too much noise and too many people, and unlike the extrovert who finds that stimulating, they need to retreat often.

In the second instance – being able to feel what others are feeling – the empath may be able to tell when others are lying, and can feel weighed down by the emotions that others are experiencing in their presence. They may sense danger, and may find violent television programmes stressful. They may be particularly sensitive to the needs of others. Google 'empath' and you'll find long lists of the empath's attributes from new age websites.

Sadly, I have to call bullshit on most, if not all, claims about so-called empaths.

First of all, like *old soul,* it doesn't make you special.

Second, if you're sensitive to what others are feeling, it's not difficult, but congratulations, your intuition is developing. You're growing up, you're not a teenager anymore, you're learning to be a caring adult. Great! We need more like you.

Third, if you can tell when people are lying, excellent. You and most police officers. Very few, if any, of whom would claim to be empaths. Again, your intuition is developing. Life does that for most of us.

Fourth. I can remember as a child and young teenager taking on the emotions of whatever was going on around me, or of whoever I was with. Children do it all the time, especially with their parents, and particularly if there's a lot of emotional tension in a home. It's not a good thing but it's the reality of our immature emotional intelligence. Mature emotional learning is to step back from others' emotions and view them separately from ourselves and *not* take them on. To continue to be taking on others' emotions as an adult is to not have grown up. To think this is a good thing is to inflict damage on yourself.

Other characteristics of the so-called empath can include:

- *You worry about what others think of you.* We all do that a lot of the time and we learn to do less of it as we mature.
- *You put others' needs above your own.* You and every mother on the planet. Likewise, we learn to do less of it as we mature.
- *Your emotions have made you physically ill.* Given the mind and body connection, this is most of us. If this is extreme and often, you need to get to the bottom of your extreme reactions and learn methods to step back from this. A good counsellor can assist you.
- *You have many highs and lows.* You probably need to work on those and create less extremes of emotion in your life. It's not good for you to be having these and it's entirely possible – and preferable – to create more moderation in your emotions. You can feel things deeply without reacting to them in the extreme.

The problem is: a) what you're feeling is very possibly your own emotion, not others – deal with your own stuff; and/or b) you've not learned to step aside from other emotions – a development stage of normal emotional maturity, and/or c) like probably half the population, you're an introvert – deal with it.

Empaths claim to be having an especially difficult time right now because the world is such a negative place. The truth though is that the world is just as equally, if not more, an absolutely amazing place, loaded to the gunnels with amazing things like love and excitement and passion and courage and joy.
If you're not feeling all those things,
then your *empath-ness* is a failed argument.

Sue Fitzmaurice

None of this is meant to undermine the very real and important characteristic of being and becoming *empathic*. But the correct meaning of this should be to *understand* others' emotions, not to feel them for oneself. Ironically though, I've found many a so-called empath to be frightfully short on empathy. I recently spent three days on a retreat with a woman who claimed often to be very empathic – by which she meant she was an empath – but every time anyone in our group expressed how they were feeling, she had a bigger story to tell. That's not empathic. That's a long way from empathic. Real empathy listens, cares, holds space, and doesn't judge.

If in your ascending spiritual vibration, you find yourself picking up on others' emotions more and more – this does happen and can affect us massively – please understand that this is not necessarily a positive thing and you need to learn methods to protect your own energy.

'Religion is wrong'

The major Abrahamic and Eastern religions are laden with truth and beauty. Religion is not a lie, nor any kind of antithesis to the truth. The notion that it is an opposite to spirituality, that one is solely dogma whereas the other is freedom, is also a lie. Religion is not an ignorance promulgated by our less evolved ancestors any more than spirituality is a modern expression of a more advanced understanding. The idea that to be spiritual entails the rejection of religion is an ignorance and one of a million examples of our inability to discern good from bad and adjust to new knowledge by throwing the baby out with the bathwater.

A prime example is the removal of Christian education from public schools. Looking back on the few memories I have of it from primary school, I recall it as a poor reflection on the teachings of Christ. But I would have preferred they were kept and been added to with instruction from the other major faith traditions *and* aspects of spiritual knowledge – meditation, for example. Instead we left our schools – and our children – devoid of vast swathes of civilisation and culture; a richness, the absence of which I fear is a colossal gap in our children's learning.

The idea that spirituality doesn't exist within religion is absurd. I'm not a fan of dogma, and much of religion has too much of it and it is without doubt a failing. The spiritual very often make up for its lack in their own ways however, creating a rigidity around their spirituality that turns their beliefs into a religion in everything but name. I've seen spirituality as dogmatic as religion, and flexibility in religion that belies its spiritual critics. Christianity is two thousand years old and has changed in a million different ways in that time – to suggest it's not flexible or open is obviously incorrect.

I've spent time around and within many religions and religious traditions. In most cases, my quest for more knowledge, for personal growth and spiritual development, has been openly supported. The exception has been within fundamentalist Christianity, where I felt any such quest was much more circumspect and was even discouraged. Conversely, it's been within some spiritual arenas that I've often felt judged, condescended to, and even shut down.

The mystical traditions within all of the world's major faiths are from where much of modern spirituality has emerged, and the depth of their wisdom and scripture holds untold treasure for those with the patience and inclination to examine them. Everything I know from the centre of religion – from their prophets and their scripture – has a spirituality at its core that is as sublime as it is subtle.

Much of what passes for religion has some horrific weaknesses, generally as it is misinterpreted and/or espoused by the religious ruling classes with a desire to manipulate and control, often with the backing of the political ruling classes of the moment. It does indeed become *an opiate of the masses* in its fear-based promulgation of whatever inequalities suit its leaders as a distraction from their own excesses. That isn't the religion – that's its leadership. To think otherwise would be the same as me decrying the United States as a despicable country because its administration is corrupt. The United States is a magnificent country and the majority of its many millions of citizens are as wonderful a people as any country's main population of ordinary, everyday folk. Much of its current administration is corrupt – not all of it, but much of it – and it's having a deleterious effect on the nation's own unique brilliance and indeed the world. But there's no value to saying the United States is a terrible country any more than there is to saying any other country is either.

Some people's commitment to their spiritual life is to find comfort in one set of principles and beliefs and stay there. There can be wisdom in that. There's also safety. There may or may not be growth. It's a choice. Don't fool yourself with your spirituality by rejecting religion in favour of another set of principles and beliefs that you also stay comfortably within – you have simply replaced one religion with another.

A great many of the world's current spiritual leaders are practitioners of religion, many of them Buddhist, others Hindu, Christian and of other faiths: the Dalai Lama, Archbishop Desmond Tutu, Mother Meera, Pema Chodron; the list is long. There are as many spiritual leaders without religion, but most have grown up with and learned from one or more religious traditions. They are all bright lights. They are joyful proponents of love. To deny the depth and beauty of the religious traditions from which they have sprung is to deny the truth and reality of their shining examples to us all. Don't be that dumb.

'You're special'

You're not.

Everyone is!

This is one of those concepts where people are oddly and rather ridiculously polarised. Who's not seen posts on social media where older generations decry the notion of rewarding children for the things they do because it's making them spoilt? As if the current younger generation don't have enough to deal with (so many things we never had), we're going to beat them up for thinking they're special as well.

Equally or more prevalent are the posts telling us all how special we are, that our voice and story are unique, that there's no one like us in the whole world, and so on. And it's true. But it's not quite the right point.

The most valuable point to make is that we're *all* unique and amazing. If we don't grasp the extraordinariness of *all* of us, then we won't actually fully grasp our own extraordinariness. Like so many of the ideas and principles here, it's a question of a) balance, and b) perspective, and by the latter I mean to say that this is something that looks different when looked at from different angles, and it's useful to try and look at it from all those different points of view – or at least more than one.

You are amazing. You are a beautiful soul with talents you may not even know about yet. You are here to spread your awesomeness around. I'm also amazing. And I'm here to spread my awesomeness around too. And we're both here to find, look at, admire, and learn from each other's brilliance.

'Be happy'

You don't have to be happy all the time.

If you are happy all the time, that's great. But don't pretend to be happy when you're not. There's an argument for faking it as a tool for learning happiness, but it's only one of several techniques, and self-awareness – knowing what it is that's making you unhappy – should be front and centre.

I've seen some very angry people faking happiness who really ought to be letting that shit go. And I've seen some very 'sweetness and light' people who'll stab you in the back quick as look at you. Authentic happiness is generous and kind and it doesn't pretend. An authentically happy person isn't happy *all* the time – they're more often than not able to a) recognise when they're not happy, and b) examine and express their unhappiness, probably without getting stuck in whatever their particular non-happiness is about at any given point. They figure it out and move on.

If you're on a spiritual path and you're unhappy, that's okay. Keep your heart and mind open and you will heal and you will get to happiness, I promise you. It takes time. If you've been unhappy for a long time, you can't undo all of that quickly.

And if your spiritual journey brings you much joy and then all of a sudden you find yourself miserable, know that there is rarely a spiritual path that is unaccompanied somewhere along the way by pain.

There is no coming to consciousness without pain.
People will do anything, no matter how absurd,
in order to avoid facing their own soul.
One does not become enlightened
by imagining figures of light,
but by making the darkness conscious.

Carl Jung

Sometimes the joy itself brings the pain, and sometimes the pain is there to herald the joy. Emotional pain can be a signpost pointing towards some part of ourselves that needs healing. You don't need to dwell there interminably but nor should you ignore it by faking happiness.

One of the biggest problems with the *be happy* scenario is that a lot of spiritual people will use it to judge others. If you're not being happy then you're infecting everyone with your negativity. Hooey. If you're struggling and you need to express what you're struggling with and other people can't handle that, that's their problem, not yours. Don't gloss over your pain because of someone else's sensitivity.

There's a common quote you'll see around social media that *holding onto anger is like drinking poison.* It's often poorly applied to encourage people to suppress their anger. This is a false interpretation of this teaching. In fact the opposite is true: don't *sup*press your anger – *ex*press it! That's how you stop holding onto it. The suppression of natural human emotions is not a path to spirituality – expressing them is. Artificially repressing some emotions with an insistence on happiness is inauthentic and will inevitably bite you in the arse.

'Namaste'

I bow to the divine in you.

A lot of greetings are given supposedly as a blessing and in the name of peace and love. Many such invocations are an ego façade of judgement and the sub-text is in reality more unfriendly. Such greetings are often given as some kind of test – if you reply with the same greeting, you've passed. It's yet another way of feeling superior.

When I'm in India, I say *Namaste* to everyone. It's what you say in India instead of *Hi* or *Hello,* especially in the villages. I've spent enough time there that it springs to my lips in greeting without even thinking about it. When I'm in London, it never enters my head.

If you've trained yourself to greet everyone with *Namaste* such that it's the first thing that springs to mind, bully for you. You go for it. But why did you do that? Because the reality is that it will cause discomfort in a large number of people you meet, so it's hardly a humble greeting of *I bow to the divine in you,* is it. In truth, it doesn't really mean this most of the time in India – mostly it's just about saying *Hello*.

Even in spiritual type settings – a retreat, say – it can be a condescension from a retreat leader or other participants. I challenge those for whom this is a common greeting to in fact say *I bow to the divine in you* when they meet someone instead. It's pretty hard to say that from a point of superiority. Make people feel good about themselves, not bad or guilty or self-conscious.

Bullshit Behaviour

Spirituality – and certainly religion, as is often mentioned – can account for vast amounts of insult and injury in the world. No one's bad behaviour can be fully blamed on their religion or their spirituality or beliefs; it's mostly just bad behaviour and as an adult you're obliged to accept responsibility for it yourself. You may or may not be obliged to accept responsibility for the harm it causes as well.

To be fair, people's behaviour is very often to do with how they feel about themselves – I don't *have* to be upset by your bad behaviour and to be so is as much my responsibility, but nevertheless our behaviours can harm others.

Anthony de Mello has a lot of wise words on authentic spirituality. He was a Jesuit priest and psychotherapist, which has always seemed to me to be a valuable combination. Raised in India, his books draw on traditions of both East and West, another valuable combination. One of the many tenets of his teachings was that it was far better to accept that we are entirely self-interested beings, and that when we understand this it makes much of life a lot clearer. It means that we can become unaffected by both the praise *and* the criticism of others, instead of behaving, as he puts it, like monkeys who react to every pull of their tail.

I press a button and you're up; I press another button and you're down. And you like that. How many people do you know who are unaffected by praise or blame? That isn't human, we say. Human means that you have to be a little monkey, so everybody can twist your tail, and you do whatever you ought to be doing. But is that human? If you find me charming, it means that right now you're in a good mood, nothing more.

Anthony de Mello

The spiritual journey should (I hate to 'should' people, but sometimes it's unavoidable) take you in the direction of being *less* affected by others, not more. Perversely, it seems most often to have the reverse impact. Our beliefs become principles by which we judge others and find them wanting, and so we become offended whenever anyone else's actions don't align with our principles. As a result we spend more time distraught at the actions of others than we do at developing our own character and spiritual alignment. We become monkeys, allowing our tails to be pulled and being eternally distracted by this, rather than becoming mature adult humans capable of keeping our tails to ourselves and controlling our own reactions.

> When you do not seek or need approval,
> you are at your most powerful.
>
> *Caroline Myss*

That said, there's a lot of bullshit behaviour among the spiritually-proclaimed that's generally a cause for concern, either because a) it's bullshit – ie. inauthentic, and/or b) it can be very harmful to both ourselves and others. Here's a selection.

Watch that sweetness, your anger is showing

Believe the anger – the sweetness is an act.

Sweet has never been a thing anyone's called me. It's not a quality of mine, although in later life I'd like to think I've moved a little further in its direction. My daughter is sweet – she's always been sweet and she's always been considered sweet by most people who know her.

What is sweetness? I think it's a certain type of lightness. It's almost a kind of innocence, although not really. The few people I've known in my life that have the kind of sweetness my daughter has, are, like Ruby, very grounded, and have an openness that is accepting of others – a readiness to love anyone that comes into their space. I think it also includes a vulnerability of sorts. It has an integrity around it – a raw and simple honesty.

I've met other people for whom I feel sweetness is an act. I see other things glaring through their veil of sweetness: anger, manipulation, backbiting, and an inherent ability to stab others in the back.

If for one second you feel like someone's sweetness is false, then it almost certainly is. I think it's one of the few gut reactions that you can really easily trust. Sweetness, like humility, cannot be forced – it comes as an innate quality. You can't fake it till you make it. Lots of other things you can – courage, creativity, even compassion and friendliness – you can summon these into your being by literally practising them. But you can't really do that with sweetness. You can try to be *nice*, but that's not the same thing.

When people fake sweetness, they also tend to gloss over things that are anything but sweet, with a veneer. This is different from trying to be positive in the face of crisis or anguish. There's a difference between recognising and accepting something's crap and trying to maintain a certain steadfastness in one's outlook, and on the other hand pretending the shit's not there at all. Nor is it to be mistaken for the ability many good people have to be polite and courteous in the face of unpleasantness either. Good for those people, I say – we could all do with more of that.

No, false sweetness hides the bearer's own anger and unpleasantness. We also know it as *passive aggression,* and it doesn't require a lot of experience in the world to recognise. To be honest I'd really rather see the bearer's angst in full flame and for that person to *own* that they're feeling that way. Then I feel like I'm dealing with a real person.

Don't pretend sweetness. It's kinda ugly. And a wee bit scary.

Do show your vulnerability though. Being open and honest in this way creates more powerful connection with those around you. It's the most courageous act of being human. This is real authenticity. And when you're authentic, some people won't like you. But that's fine.

And be weird. Being your own strange self is real and will develop your other virtues quicker than anything else. Don't hide any of your unique you – be your very best imperfect self.

A proviso: your uncontrolled anger is also out of place and nobody owes you the time or place to unleash it.

It's not your triggers, it's your bad behaviour

We all get triggered. To be triggered means that you react instinctively to things others say and do, and we use the term when that reaction is negative. (We don't tend to say we've been triggered into being happy.) For example, if you were violently assaulted, seeing this happen on the television may trigger you and you might react, say, with fear or panic. If you're aware you can have this reaction then you might take steps to avoid that kind of exposure, or there may be things you do to reduce your fear and panic when it arises, and all of that is appropriate. If instead you turn your reaction onto someone else in such a way that you harm them, that's not appropriate. And knowing that you were triggered is not an acceptable excuse.

Here's another example. Your husband once had an affair. In a discussion with other women someone mentions that they have some compassion for women who end up in affairs with married men because those women have often been lied to as much as the wife has been. Objectively it's not an unreasonable point. If you, as the woman whose husband has had an affair, shoot down in flames the woman that expresses this opinion, you've been triggered. There's obviously a case for claiming women shouldn't have affairs with married men, and it would be right to say so in such a conversation, but here's the thing: 1) You're in a conversation with friends – maybe you're out to lunch together or some other social setting – don't shoot people down in flames for expressing a reasonable view; 2) Few things are black and white; 3) Even if they're wrong, there are ways of explaining that and/or handling it, and barking at someone is generally not the way; 4) The woman isn't saying it's right – she's expressing sympathy for women who are lied to, period. And 5), most importantly, you need to manage your triggers, not make someone else responsible for them.

How do you know when you're triggered? If you can't be reasonable in expressing your point of view, then you may well have been triggered. If you're feeling outraged, if your pulse is beating harder, if you feel like yelling at someone, then you've been triggered. And if you know all this and you use this as an excuse for subsequent poor behaviour then you're out of line. And you know what else? You're continuing to make yourself a victim of whatever it was that happened to you that caused that reaction in you. And any time you make a victim of yourself you are disempowering yourself.

This isn't about not being angry about things that really are unreasonable. Like any humane person, I can be upset seeing harm inflicted on others. We're assailed with these things daily – animal abuse, child abuse, wars, the crisis of refugees, abuses of power, bigotry, the list goes on and on. Potentially there could be something among those that triggers me, because maybe I've had something similar happen to me. My responsibility is to take stock of my reaction and manage it, not to turn my upset emotions onto someone else. (And I can also choose to do something constructive to better or alleviate those situations rather than complain about them. But that's another issue.)

Sadly, this notion of being triggered is something I hear a lot from people in spiritual arenas, often from those with the privilege of guiding others. Not okay.

Your triggers are never an excuse for behaving badly, especially towards others. We all have them – you can choose to let them define you, or you can use them as fodder for your personal growth.

The arrogant expert

There's not knowing much, and then there's not knowing much and being a dick about it. And when it comes to spiritual matters, the one talking the most and the loudest is very often the one that knows the least, especially if they're putting others down in the process. The one who knows the most may very well be quieter, less likely to be assertive about it, and has more questions than answers. *The more I learn, the less I know* is a truism for the wise.

Far greater wisdom – or opportunity to learn – may be discovered with the humble, the quiet, and the reserved among us, and I'm increasingly motivated to seek out those individuals.

The arrogant expert – who isn't generally an expert, but we'll keep calling them that just the same – is probably charismatic and charming, and may have the ability to draw others into their orbit. In spiritual circles this is often an attractive younger male, and he could be surrounded by preening older women.

A friend relayed a story from a spirituality expo where a young man had a roomful of middle-aged women chanting *Yoooooo-neeeeeee* in an exercise designed to engage with their personal divine feminine. She knew most of them didn't know what *yoni* was.

Small point, but it's almost never a good idea to seek advice on any aspect of being a woman from a man (unless he's your gynaecologist and then only in terms of your physical body). On almost any other topic for sure, but not that one.

More than anything, beware the expert that espouses principles that he or she then uses as a standard by which they judge you. A true teacher will offer you what they know and allow you to take what you will. They won't be attached to what you agree with or not – theirs is just to teach, and their attitude is one of sharing. They will probably even be interested to hear from you just as much as they seek to impart their own wisdom. They are not offended by any lack of regard on your part for what they espouse, and will either gently engage with you on your beliefs or not at all.

One of the greatest challenges for the newly awakened, or newly spiritually aware individual, is that in the vast swathe of spiritual information there are a lot of people offering some horrific misinterpretations of spiritual teachings. Given the abundance of spiritual teachings available, even the more experienced among us can be at a loss sometimes to determine authenticity from falsehood, truth from fraud. And so the amateur is at huge risk of being taken in, especially by the charming, charismatic, arrogant expert, who may even feign a type of humility to accompany their act. Sadly, the amateur may then also proclaim a knowledge that is realistically beyond their limited introduction to this new world of spirituality. Whilst this is commonly seen within fundamentalist religions (of which most religions have at least an element), particularly among younger adherents, it's common enough also in the spiritual arena. It's often less obvious since it's not so institutionalised and you're less likely to see it en masse, but it's equally there.

Be mindful of the teaching you seek or follow and the credentials or validity of any teacher. Maintain some objectivity in all elements of your journey.

Angry vegans

Angry vegans, angry Christians, angry environmentalists, angry anyone. If a message is led by anger (and generally equal parts self-righteousness), it's less true. The words may come from a truth but find someone who's saying them without the accompanying anger. If, behind the words, you sense hate and/or judgement of others, better to find someone who's speaking them without that accompanying baggage. Fear, hate, anger and judgement are the world's greatest diseases. They offer no solutions to the world's ills and to the extent that they are behind much supposedly righteous words and actions, they are not useful. Doctrine projected on a foundation of fear and hate and anger has no place in the world today. They speak louder than the righteousness of any words or actions ever can, and they serve only to generate more of the same.

There are a few exceptions to this. Greta Thunberg's address to press at the United Nations in late 2019 was famously angry. I didn't have a problem with that. There is some righteous anger that's justifiable. And Greta wasn't rallying anyone else to hatred – her aim was to provoke action among world leaders and she's been very effective.

I understand that we can all easily be angry about a lot of things. I can be angry about selfishness; I'm angry about the politics of fear; I hate war; and I can be judgemental about arrogant loudmouths. And to some extent I'm probably right to be angry. But it's not useful to express one's rage. Leapfrog your anger into not liking something enough to do something about it. Or shut up. Most righteous anger only serves to propagate more anger, and the world has had enough of that repetitive cycle. Do something about the things you want to change in the world and do it with love. It's the only way.

Anger causes cancer and it is a cancer.

It's so easy to go there though. Remind yourself, and your friends and loved ones, when anger comes, let it go with love and turn it into loving action.

Most of all, don't give credence to the spiritual teacher if you sense underlying fear or hate or anger – their words are tinged with it and it's not worth taking them in. Always find the softer way.

And for God's sake don't now descend upon your cancer-suffering relative with a declaration of their anger-causing tumour. You can't throw people's anger back in their faces – that's an aggressive act with no positive outcome. Just love them. Shower them with love and affection.

The bubble of righteousness

If you've made your spirituality a religion, you've quite possibly created a bubble around you that you won't venture out of, and you won't allow anything else in. Probably you've decorated your bubble with rainbows to make it seem the perfect bubble. It's not – it's just a bubble.

Inside your bubble, you don't allow anything in that doesn't fit perfectly with your spiritual décor. If it has a different view, a different way of speaking, a different accent, different clothes, then you don't want it to corrupt your carefully laid-out theme. I've got news for you: you've got spiritual xenophobia. And you're possibly an arsehole.

I had a member of my extended family whose hippy goal in life used to be to get through life without ever having to wear socks or underwear. Since he worked outdoors in winter, he had to eventually give up on the socks part of the goal. (Yes, I'm totally judging him.) He would trumpet loudly that his body was his temple, among his many proclamations. He'd do things like open my fridge to get milk for his tea and proclaim that *this soy milk is shit!* When I announced to our family that I was pregnant with my second child not long after having suffered a miscarriage, he went off on a tirade about over-population, I reached my limit of polite tolerance. He was self-righteous about everything – and remains so – and it's exhausting. He had a perfect spiritual décor and he expected everyone else to have it too.

Self-righteousness is ugly. It pushes people away, it has no love or kindness in it, and it's an almost impossible behaviour to counter with any kind of logic. It puts up walls and it isolates. It cannot hear any other point of view. The bubble resident is truthfully in a dark, walled-up cave.

Judging others

Being spiritual means nothing if you can't be nice to everyone, including those you consider less spiritually developed than you (which is not something you should spend much time considering, to be fair, since everyone's path is different). If you're not fundamentally focused on being unconditionally loving to all living things, you're not fundamentally focused on being spiritual.

Don't be in a hurry to condemn a person because he doesn't do what you do, or think as you think. There was a time when you didn't know what you know today.

Malcolm X

We all judge lots of people for lots of things lots of the time. And it's extremely difficult to stop it. *Everybody* is different from us, has different opinions, different values, and different ways of doing things. We can *always* find something to disagree on with just about anyone. But what would be the point?

There are reasons we make judgements about others, principle among them that we're insecure and/or jealous. If you're comfortable with who you are and what you have, then there's no need to judge anyone else.

> ## The ability to observe without evaluating
> ## is the highest form of intelligence.
>
> *Jiddu Krishnamurti*

I'm not talking here about situations where people have actually done something wrong, ie. against the law. That situation will hopefully be judged by the proper legal process. I'm talking about making judgements about how people look, what they wear, their opinions. You can disagree with their opinions, albeit hopefully within a process that involves you actually engaging with them and finding out more about their opinions. But to decide that a person is 'less than' because of their opinions or how they look or behave, should always be unacceptable to the spiritual seeker. (Frequently we make these judgements about people we don't even know!)

The harm caused by judging others can be catastrophic. Our judgements wound our victims, even when they don't know about them – if they know about them, it's even worse of course. You add to the collective negative shit in the world with your judgements and you are likely perpetuating stereotypes: about what women should look like, about what's spiritual and what's not, about the right ways to behave in certain situations, and on and on.

Significantly though, we harm ourselves. In truth, no one feels good about the judgements they make about others. Maybe for a moment, but then it's gone and it's replaced by guilt.

Judgement is an act of ego; firstly in the making of it, and secondly in the sticking to it. Because we all like to stick to some of our worse judgements come hell or high water. Out of guilt we will talk about our harshest judgements with others and try to get them to agree with us. And once we've convinced one or two people, we'll feel less guilty for a while. We ringfence our judgement with the reinforcements of other people, keeping our harshest judgements in place, ensuring they continue to do harm. We ignore that our judgement is creating suffering: to its victim, to ourselves, and to the world. Because *godammit,* we're right!

What a sad, sorry state of affairs.

If you're sincere about your spiritual path, you'll need to deal to your judging nature. It's one of the single greatest obstacles to spiritual growth and does not serve you in any way – indeed it harms you.

> ## Once you awaken, you will have no interest
> ## in judging those who sleep.
>
> *James Blanchard*

We've all got battles others can neither see nor understand. There'll be times you'll want the world to treat you kindly despite your grumpiness or despite your temper – give others the same respect. And then consider where your judgement is coming from:

- o Do you understand that person's reality?
- o Have you got unfair or unrealistic expectations of others?
- o Do you think you're better than them?
- o Does their situation in fact invoke some vulnerability in you?

Two important things to do: 1. Sit with your judgements and get to the bottom of where they're coming from in you. 2. Put yourself in the other person's shoes a while. Seeing the world through their eyes will help expand your own world, as well as your compassion.

Finally, if you don't heal what's wounded you, you will bleed on people who didn't hurt you.

Bitches, and other spiritual people who shit on you

I'm not sure if I've possibly met more bitches in the spiritual world than in the corporate world, or which is worse. Sad to say, one expects to have to deal with nasty women in the corporate world but it's so disappointing to find them in the spiritual world. I've been shat on, spat on and sat on by so many – I've been lied to, stabbed in the back, betrayed, and had several tons of someone else's crap thrown at me. The ability of 'spiritual' women to analyse one's personality, one's strengths and weaknesses, to such a detailed level, tell everyone about it – including you – can be so vicious and so harming. In this world you can be scorned for your success more than any other, torn down for your beliefs, and have your energy and aura spiritually analysed to within an inch of its awesomeness. I've seen women swarm around the most viciously harmful among them to protect them from invisible demons, and I've seen brutally narcissistic women call up swarms of spiritual drones among their friends to brutalise other women. I've never known gossip like it. I once heard gossip about myself second-hand, via two people who didn't know me, that had gone across three countries to get to me. It's enough to make you want to go in your cave and never come out. But you do come out, and you look at yourself carefully and closely, because that's what you feel obliged to do on this path, and you grieve and you hurt and you feel like a victim; until you've worked through it a thousand times, hopefully with the help of loving friends who *do* care about you, and you get to the end of all that and if you're lucky you still feel okay about yourself. And you let go the pain and send the bitches on their way. With love. Or not. And you're stronger and wiser and more resilient and more loving. And you begrudgingly might thank the bitches for the lesson. Or not. And maybe you think about Mary Magdalene being called a prostitute for two millennia, and Mother Mary losing her precious son and then being forgotten about, and the tens of thousands of witches burnt for healing the sick, and on it goes, and you wonder at all the people who reject religion for spirituality only to behave in the same dire ways. And if you don't let it all completely do your head in, you get out of bed another day and meditate and open your heart and offer what you have to your family and friends and the world. The tests we receive from other people are the hardest. The people we love the most can often hurt us the most. And it can leave you utterly lost, wondering what you missed, what you got wrong, and which way is up.

Don't fuck someone over emotionally and spiritually and then walk away like nothing happened. Don't allow your spirituality to turn you into a bitch. Don't *be* a bitch, period. If your spiritual position allows you to behave badly towards others, especially those also operating within a spiritual domain, then your spirituality needs a good looking at. Because it's feeding you some serious bullshit. And for whatever reason, you're gobbling it up like a pig. Figure out the reason and you'll figure out the next thing you need to be working on in your spiritual journey. Cruelty does not become the seeker.

Over-spiritualising

People who over-spiritualise have a spiritual answer for everything. Not feeling well? Your chakras must be blocked. Struggling financially? You must be clearing karma from past lives. And my all-time favourite, whenever *anything* happens: It's a sign!

Some of these answers may be correct, but they're very often not useful. They can create guilt in someone, making them feel 'less than', and inducing them to spend perhaps vast sums of money on often questionable recovery methods. Less than half-arsed, so-called spiritual explanations for whatever ails someone can quickly create a new spiritual junkie flitting from one possible solution to another, and is at the root of a mega-billion dollar spiritual industry that keeps a lot of very amateur and inexperienced 'practitioners' in a manner to which they'd like to become accustomed.

There are indeed energy solutions for most of our problems, but we need to be wary of becoming stuck in our spiritual process. The reality of spiritual growth and development is generally a lot simpler. The spiritual path doesn't have to be a mysterious one where we try to unlock the truth of every occurrence.

We can twist ourselves up in a lot of knots trying to figure out the spiritual meaning of everything that happens in our lives. I'm an expert in this. I do it as much as any other spiritual person and more than many. My spiritual path is of utmost priority for me in my life and so therefore spiritual answers are the ones I seek. Too often. For everything. Someone was a total arse to me? So what do I need to learn from this? What's going on for them? Is karma the only explanation? What karma? What is it about my energy that attracts the wrong people to me? Were they the wrong people? Maybe they were the right people. Maybe that was a lesson from the universe? What's the lesson? And on and on and on. I can do this for weeks, months and even years. It's a curse. It's apparently a particular burden of Librans, who can't stand things being unfair and who have to have answers.

There are always things to be learned. Learn them and move on. Staying too long in seeking explanations will leave your mind in an incomprehensible turmoil that will trap you in uncertainty and act as an obstacle to moving forward on the next part of your journey. It's a bit like exam technique: if you can't think of the answer, move onto the next one and come back to it later if you have time.

There are also legitimate physical and emotional reasons – and solutions – for much of what ails us, and we ignore these at our peril. Whether or not you believe you're a spiritual being in a physical body, the fact of that physical body and this physical world remains and it's foolish to ignore them.

Finally, don't be going around spiritually diagnosing everyone else. Any worthy practitioner knows that they must be asked and given permission before they may do so. See: *Judging others.*

Spiritual addictions

I'm not sure I've met the person without some kind of addiction. I have several drugs of choice myself: food, nicotine (I vape now), binge television, social media. Probably there's more. In the past it's also been work, money, power (such as I had), and various other things. We can easily replace one with another.

Addictions are all about finding relief from the pain of life; they're our go-to to make ourselves feel better. But every addiction has a sting in its tail that undermines the feel-good factor, in the shorter or longer term. And they're a quick fix; by definition they get in the way of us doing something more substantial and meaningful to make a difference in our lives.

Spiritual addicts come in different varieties. There are those whose ego is so tied up in their spirituality that they can't see God for all the doctrine they've put around Him/Her. They can be exceptionally judgemental of others, sadly more often those whose hearts are gentle and open and who are seeking. The worst of these addicts engage in a level of criticism and hate that is, ultimately, like any other addiction, highly self-destructive, although not before (also like a lot of addictions) tearing other people down as well. They try to get you to think as they do, often ceaselessly.

Another type of spiritual addict is on an endless pursuit of the spiritual high. Some aspects of fundamentalism feed this. Loud singing, chanting, cheering, a-whoopin' an' a-hollerin', create an adrenaline-fueled experience that can make the believer feel they're filled with the spirit and doing God's holy work, when really they may have just been stirred up into plain old excitement. This is not to deny the very real experiences of the spirit, and the great value of creating joy, but the young convert will likely not know the difference between all of these.

Other spiritual addicts constantly search for the next possible answer (and the next and the next) to life's problems. Course junkies are like this. They go wide instead of deep and miss the beauty that emerges from depth and discipline and time and commitment. They go from one course to another in the hope of finding some holy grail that will finally lead to the discovery of their purpose. It's very easy to do – the next fix is there seconds after you've logged into your social media. We are bombarded with articles, posts, and memes on how to change our lives.

These are information addicts. They store vast swathes of sometimes dubious 'facts' but rarely is this alone transformative. If you're skipping across a breadth of learning without going beyond the superficial, you're unlikely to find fulfilment, and certainly not transformation.

Waking up and deciding to step onto a spiritual path is a process. Your waking up moment may have been sudden and massive, but mostly from thereon it's going to be step by step. Sometimes you can want too much, too soon. There's an urgency that many of us have at different stages where we feel like there's no time left. It's a natural response to knowing we've ignored the spiritual for most or all of our life up until now, so we compensate by throwing ourselves into it. It's a great way to lose perspective, and it undermines the vital fact that the spiritual journey doesn't have a stopwatch. It's timeless. It doesn't matter that you only just started (in this life), because the journey goes on forever, and has been going on forever up until now too.

Spiritual lessons aren't learned in a day. You need to take your time to practise and cement them into your life and into your subconscious. If you're not locking each lesson in place, they'll blow over in a half decent wind next time a crisis hits.

The addict can be one-eyed about their spiritual practice, believing there is only one way to get to where they're going. The one-path spiritual practitioner is the most deluded of all practitioners, and the single most annoying. You'll pretty much get everyone's back up around you, and your path will quickly become one of dogma rather than true spiritual seeking. A singular perspective is not a path of growth. If your path doesn't allow for different perspectives, you're not on a spiritual path, you're on a one-track ride to hell – a definition of hell, in my mind, being a place that excludes the joy of the breadth of real spiritual connection.

The true spiritual seeker entertains ambiguity. If you're operating without doubt, or you're single-mindedly rejecting it, then you're probably operating from fear – fear that you'll be diverted from your 'one true path'. Spiritual joy and harmony, by definition, are not born out of fear. Fear does not manifest love. It manifests things that are entirely counter to love, like indifference and anger and hate and judging others. Let your doubts in, ponder them, talk about them with a learned teacher – one who operates without fear and is happy to discuss your uncertainty with you. It may be that your misgivings will lead you to something amazing that will take you into new and beautiful realms of learning and wonder.

If you can see yourself here – a potential addict – do yourself a favour and take a break. Step back. Look around. Look at what others are doing, ask questions, experiment a little, read a lot. It's okay. You're not going to lose yourself – you were very possibly on a path to doing that when you thought you were being disciplined and focused. Maybe you'll re-focus your efforts back to that particular practice, but don't be afraid to put a little space around it for a while.

Spirituality isn't about getting a fix. Every junkie's addiction will eventually get the better of them and inhibit their elevation.

Polarisation

There is *way* too much black and white in our everyday lives, and very little of it is helpful.

In the political sphere, we see huge divides between the left and right in most countries in the world, much of it increasingly extreme, especially that which we now call the far right. Much of this portion of the political spectrum vote not only against their own best interests but also against those of most of the world. Witness the bizarre adherence to an anti-climate change belief despite massive exposure to the scientific evidence. And as a portion of society, this demographic also demonstrates horrific xenophobia, racism, sexism and every other kind of 'ism.

If you believe all of the world's scientists got together to fake 7,000 climate studies as part of an elaborate hoax, you're not a conservative, you're a lunatic.

We have to stop treating people brainwashed by right-wing propaganda as political actors and start treating them as patients.

Cenk Uygur

What used to be generally the middle of the political spectrum is now portrayed by the far right as being the far left, which in fact it is not, but it's very difficult to position oneself in the middle when a significant section of society is racing to the cliff's edge on the right. As reasonable people resist the pull towards disaster, they find themselves increasingly expressive of their community values, and without necessarily wanting to be they become activists for what had always seemed normal. It is a fundamental of conflict resolution that to the extent that one party pulls to an extreme, the other party has no choice but to dig their heels in too. Moderation is not possible. Thus, polarisation.

The same picture of a chasm exists in the spiritual and religious communities between some groups' views and other groups' views.

The more interesting and problematic polarisation in spiritual and religious communities is a different type of polarisation. It's the insistence on certain things being right or wrong, good or bad. To the extent that this situation overlays the political one, it makes for even greater polarisation in each sphere.

I'm not talking about the polarisation around beliefs – whether there is a God or not, and whether Jesus is the only way or just another enlightened teacher – I could go on and on and on about those differences and they're not important. I'm talking about the idea that when we screw up, we're a screw-up; or that when we make a mistake, we've done it all wrong. There is nothing limits us on our spiritual path more than judging, or being judged for, our actions. Right and wrong, good and bad, are relative terms on one's spiritual journey, and you can't always determine one from the other. This isn't to deny the value of wisdom, or that some spiritual choices will be more fruitful than others. But 'wrong' and 'bad' are rarely if ever of value.

From the physical perspective, most of you believe that your beliefs are the right ones, and that if you disagree with someone then they must be wrong. But from the non-physical view, it is not seen as 'right' and 'wrong'. It is seen as a powerful diversity that stimulates thought, and you should enjoy that diversity.

From the wisdom of Abraham Hicks

Be mindful of the spiritual path that proclaims too much about right and wrong, or good and bad; it has potential to pull you into extremes that won't serve you.

Spiritual 'splaining

I love seeing 'mansplaining' called out. Twitter is brilliant for this. Like the Joe Blow that tried to explain space to a woman astronaut, or the nob[1] that told a woman she needed to read the whole article that she'd actually written. It's about less qualified men assuming more qualified women need help understanding things. It's intellectual manspreading and it makes a right twat[2] of its protagonist.

Spiritual 'splaining is an ill-advised activity undertaken by a newbie and inflicted upon someone for whom the proffered wisdom is already well understood and even passé. It's likely to be accompanied by a lot of should's and ought to's.

If the 'splaining hasn't got completely on their tits, the recipient will generally just smile. It's a particular and unmistakeable smile, and if you're in the habit of 'splaining, you should look out for it. Sadly though, most 'splainers are oblivious to it. 'Splainers are muppets.[3] Don't be a 'splainer.

---

[1] British insult meaning a foolish person.

[2] British insult meaning a foolish person.

[3] British insult meaning a foolish person.

Other Bullshit

Blaming the universe

I invoke the power of the universe frequently. It's a mindset that has to do with a belief in something bigger than myself that I'm nonetheless inherently a part of. Being a part of it means intrinsically that it influences what happens in my life. I tend to use *the Universe* as a euphemism for God. I personally don't have a problem with the idea of God, but a lot of people do and so I've got in the habit of saying *the Universe* instead. And anyway, it has a different feel to it – it's, well, more universal. It's got more dimensions to it, it's not gendered. The universe is the universe, but what's God? I have my idea of God, but yours is probably different. The problem is though, as with God, the universe gets the blame for way too much.

It's not responsible for my life and everything that happens to me. I can't go around blaming it for the crap in my life any more than I can make it responsible for the good stuff that comes my way either. Of course, there is an argument for doing just that, but *it's not useful.* If we make the universe responsible for everything, we make ourselves responsible for nothing, and not only is that false but it's an obstacle to learning and it's disempowering.

The thing is that the spiritual argument for blaming the universe, as much as the practical one, is false. I believe I'm a spiritual being and I believe the universe is fundamentally spiritual and that I'm a part of it. I believe I have a higher self, my spiritual self, that connects me to the larger realm of the spirit world. Because of that connection, I'm potentially all-powerful. Of course, in actuality I don't yet appear to be, but the potential exists from the spiritual perspective and I'm all good with that.

It is precisely because of that connection though that nothing comes into my world that I've not allowed in or invited in myself, whether I'm aware of it or not. So the universe is not bloody responsible – I am! What's more, nine times out of ten, in the practical world I'm also responsible.

It's true that possibly I didn't get that job because it wasn't *meant to be* or because the universe *has something better lined up for me*, but I also didn't get it because a) there was someone else more suited than me, and/or b) I didn't interview as well, or prepare as well, as I could have.

Maybe some of the shit in your life happened because you made some bad decisions. It's not beyond the realms of possibility. I had a friend who decided to totally pack up his life and career in one country and move lock, stock and barrel to another, with the intention of building a new business there. Pretty much everything that could go wrong went wrong. His relationship suffered, the business didn't take off with the speed he'd hoped, his house in his native country didn't sell, and there were numerous legal problems. The insanity was that he didn't just do this once – he did it three times, moving to three different countries. Each time believing it would work this time. Was it running away? Quite possibly. Did the universe have other plans? Possibly that too. Did he make hasty and wrong decisions? Almost definitely. Did he listen to advice? Virtually none. And throughout this period, which lasted at least a few years, everything was blamed on the universe. Everything.

I am all for following your dreams and I'm all for jumping in, taking the leap, throwing caution to the winds and trusting the universe to lend support. In fact, I believe the universe fronts up more when we take great leaps. I tell my clients *Give the universe something to play with* and it will come out to play. I take my hat off to people who do that; I've done it myself. It takes balls. But! Plan, think, and most of all, take responsibility. You're in partnership with the universe, and like any good relationship one party doesn't get to make all the decisions and then only blame the other party when it all goes pear-shaped.

Trite comments like *It's meant to be* and *The universe has something better coming your way* are not helpful. They take power away from us. *I* have something better lined up for me. Me! *I'm* in charge of my life. *I'm* going to make it happen. As for *It's meant to be*... how the hell do you know what's *meant to be* in someone else's life? You don't know that. I don't even know that and it's my life. Maybe it was meant to be and maybe it wasn't. Either way, it's not useful. What if I got the job but it turned out to be shit? That's happened to me before today too. Was that meant to be? I don't bloody know.

In the end, the universe in fact guides us through our lives in the gentlest way possible. Sometimes 'gentle' can seem a bit rough admittedly – sometimes obstacles need to be cleared in order to live our best lives.

The universe doesn't deliver you crap as blessings. If it delivers anything, it delivers blessings as blessings. Most of what happens though is either just life, or you fucked up. Either way, should you decide to examine what lessons lie in the things that come your way, good for you. Always a good idea. But maybe there aren't any. Maybe it was just a piece of shit that turned up because life is like that sometimes.

You decide what's shit and what isn't. Sometimes it is a gift and you turn it into that by using it for your own cause, to be a better you. And if it could be a gift if you turned it into one, but you don't, then it's just shit. It's either manure or it stinks – you decide. And then it's *your* gift to you; *you* make it a gift.

By the same token, we can wonder what we've done to attract the shit. Maybe you didn't do anything. Maybe it just happened. If you spend too much time wondering what's wrong with you then you'll necessarily be spending less time loving yourself for being the awesome human you are. Maybe there's a lesson there, but it's possible to spend so much time analysing everything that you forget to smell the roses.

By the same token, we can tend to give the universe credit for every *good* thing that comes our way too. Or worse, we blame it for the crap but take all the credit ourselves for the good stuff.

There is always a case for the luck of having been in the right place at the right time, but you put yourself there and you made something of the opportunity that came your way. Empower yourself with your own good fortune. Don't give it away. Giving it away makes you a victim of circumstance as much as it makes you a recipient of good fortune.

The harder I work, the luckier I get.

Coleman Cox

If it feels good and makes you happy, you don't need to give responsibility for it to any player, yourself or the universe. Just enjoy it, whatever it is, but definitely don't give your power away.

I make this mistake myself. I've had a bounteous few years of travel and other experiences since I decided to leave home. I frequently express my gratitude to the universe for it all. And that's not a bad thing, but every now and then I remind myself that I worked hard to establish a life that could work that way, and that I have fairly substantial reserves of courage to be able to do what I do, frequently with fewer financial resources and very often by jumping into the unknown. And it's good to remind myself I have those characteristics – they're a part of what defines me and when I remind myself of them, I feel more empowered and powerful.

When the spiritual becomes religious

This is one of the most important points here. I see this happen over and over again. Someone lands on a spiritual truth, or a set of them, and then they stick rigidly to those truths, turning them into dogma, and fearing all other truths. That's not spirituality – that's religion. Nowhere are there more religious people than among the self-proclaimed spiritual. I frequently see more openness, flexibility, kindness and spirituality, among practitioners of actual religions than I do among those who've categorically rejected the religious for the spiritual.

If your spirituality is closed to new ideas and critical of other spiritual practices then you've become religious, which is probably something you've criticised in the past for its lack of flexibility and openness. The very definition of spiritual is that it is dynamic and moving, and there is an acknowledgement of many truths and many paths.

Doggedness must surely come from the same linguistic foundations as the word dogma, and we see this doggedness among fundamentalists of all kinds, including spiritual fundamentalists. They are as unappealing as the decidedly un-Christ-like Christians we're all familiar with.

You can't manifest everything you want

There is nothing I've seen create greater feelings of inadequacy in the spiritual world than the pressure and inability to manifest one's desires. Despite the deluge of testimonies from the newly wealthy or massively accomplished that they have mastered the art of manifesting, there remains a population a thousand times greater, for whom lack of mastery of this skill has meant feelings of shortcoming and a lack of capacity.

Fuelling this generation of spiritual ineptitude are many otherwise amazing humans unaware that their success has rendered so many others hopeless. One shining example of this is Oprah Winfrey. Oprah is exceptional, there's no doubt about it. But I was disappointed by a chink in her story when I heard her speak at an event in Auckland, New Zealand, several years ago. Her rags to riches story is inspiring, but for the most part Oprah credits her success with her own ability to manifest. In her two hour monologue, no mention was ever made of her incredible intelligence, her ability to work bloody hard, the fact that she made some very wise choices, and the simple reality of good luck. Smarts get you a long way in life, and I think not to credit them does one a disservice, and Oprah has smarts by the ton.

You can manifest a lot of what you want, especially if you've really mastered the art. But until such time, you need to be realistic, and know that it's going to take practice.

By the same token, some of the nonsense around manifesting tells us that we should never talk about anything 'negative' because otherwise we'll give rise to it, or of course simply because it's not spiritual to do so. Again, this is delusion. We must talk about what pains us if we are to move on from it. Not to, suppresses our pain and ensures that it will come back to bite us in the future, usually when we least expect it.

True spirituality requires honesty, not pretending. We're human. To masquerade as otherwise is inauthentic.

Putting all your spiritual eggs in one basket

There is huge value in spreading your spiritual curiosity across more than one teaching. Even among a single religion – Christianity, say – there are multiple perspectives: academic and mystical, conservative and liberal, traditional and modern.

Imagine the entirety of the spiritual realm is out there, beyond the atmosphere of Planet Earth. And let's say you've got one telescope to look through, but that telescope only looks in one direction, at one wee corner of the universe. That's a lot of universe you're not seeing.

If you think God is confined to your one small set of beliefs, you're forgetting that you're made in God's image, not the other way around. When you limit God to your small mind's view – by which I don't mean that you in particular are small-minded (my point is that we all are in comparison to the infiniteness of the universe) – then you've made God in *your* image, and that's not only an insult to God, but you're profoundly limiting yourself.

There are over seven billion different spiritual views in the world, and yes some are misguided if their beliefs are leading them into death and destruction, but potentially every one of those seven billion views are worth examining. We have much to learn from each other.

Placing all your attention on one teaching – or on one teacher – carries a lot of risk. You forfeit perspective and you may very well forfeit your own power. You are often your own best teacher – don't outsource your power to any single teacher or teaching.

Don't fall for someone else's idea of what you need. This is a challenging notion, because it's great to seek out expertise and advice. Myself, I think the best way to achieve that is to cast the net wide. It's not always a good idea to have *one* teacher, at least not indefinitely. There are exceptions to that, but *most* spiritual teachers you will come across aren't at the very top of their game – few of us are gurus or Rinpoches in the absolute sense of those words.

It's very easy to become infatuated with a particular friend or teacher's advice – it's another way we give up our own power. And our own perspective. The wisest friends will be sparing with advice and heavy on kindness, listening and support. Experience, your own mistakes, and the development of your intuition, will make you your own best teacher, or at least enable you to sift the wheat from the bullshit.

The best teachers will focus your attention on your own ability, not theirs.

Your one-day certificate doesn't make you an expert

I'm often suspicious of the person with a million certificates in different things. I mean really, can you do one thing well?

I understand trying out different things to see what it is that's your thing. But becoming a course junkie won't reveal your purpose in life, at least where the courses are across a breadth of topics and only at the beginner stage in terms of their depth.

A fatal error for the ardent pursuer of purpose is to keep trying lots of different things, in the hope that one of those things will leap out at you as the answer to all your purpose prayers.

This doesn't work. It can't. This is the scattergun approach to trying to find your purpose. Not only is it shallow, but the notion that we're acquiring meaning is an illusion. We may well be acquiring lots of interesting skills that in the moment feel great, but as long as you're grazing superficially across many potential opportunities, you're not going deep into any one thing, and therefore you're not really acquiring true meaning.

Course junkies do this. I've had a number of clients and friends who are course junkies. They love learning and trying new things, and I get that. I love it too. But it would also do my head in. And what I see with those who do this, is that they become so increasingly committed to this mode of pursuit that they can't stop and they lack the ability to stick with anything when it doesn't feel like the absolutely perfect thing. They miss out on the very real and life-changing challenges that come from sticking with something and going deep into it and facing up to whatever parts of ourselves we rub up against when we do that.

True pursuit of purpose is not achieved via grazing. You have to sit down to a proper meal, at the table, and take your time with what's in front of you.

(If you've seen the contradiction this section presents to the previous one, well done you!)

Of considerable concern is the spiritual or health practitioner with no other skill or experience than their one-day course 'certification'. Or frankly, the one-month course. I understand your new course may have created a clarity for you around developing a new career, and that you must begin applying it somewhere, but please continue to deepen and expand your knowledge, because you're not there yet.

Pain isn't spiritual and illness isn't your fault

We all understand that the connection between the body, mind and soul, means that we can't separate what's happening in our bodies from what must be happening in our hearts and minds. But we need to be a bit smarter – and a bit kinder – about how we take this on board.

First off, the notion of fault isn't useful. It's tied to equally damaging notions of guilt. As if you didn't have enough to deal with already, some spiritual git comes along and tells you your illness is your own fault. Lord, have mercy.

I have heaps of things wrong with me. I've hurt so many people I care about because of stupid behaviour I didn't even recognise at the time. Some of it I still don't recognise. If I could figure out where it came from, you can bet I'd be trying to fix it. All of us have lesser characteristics, bad behaviours, and crap that we don't necessarily understand the origins of. For all I know, some of it's been around through millennia of past lives. I can't figure it all out, but I am doing my best. I'd be really pissed off if I got cancer – a) it would feel really unfair, and b) I've done so much spiritual work that I would have hoped would raise my vibration away from cancer. But if I did get it, I'd be doing my damnedest to figure out precisely which bit of emotional baggage manifested that way, as well as seeking the best treatment. I swear though, if someone told me it was my own fault, I might spit at them. Even if they used a less blaming word like *responsibility*, I might still spit at them. *You've only got yourself to blame* is never of any value ever.

Illness – mental, physical or otherwise – is a part of life and manifests for any one of thousands of different reasons. Only you can assess the myriad of answers open to you, both in terms of cause and in terms of treatment. My concern here is in the messages we give ourselves and others about the spiritual nature of illness and the ways we burden ourselves unnecessarily with mind games over what we did and did not reap upon ourselves. Don't go there. And don't send anyone else there.

By the same token, pain is not spiritual, and to say so is dense. Pain is extremely physical. There is little if anything else that is more physical. Nor is its cause spiritual. Notwithstanding phenomena such as phantom pain and the like, the *cause* of pain is also most definitely physical.

There's another school of thought that makes deliberate pain a means of enlightenment. 'Our Lord suffered so we should too.' People that want to go down that road are so far from listening to anything I've got to say here that I'm not even going to try to address that particular practice. If you want to whip yourself, go for it; don't let me stop you. If you have a less fundamentalist view of suffering that nonetheless still defines it as a necessity along the spiritual path, there are a bunch of things you could think about.

One. Pain – physical and emotional – is a part of life. There is a vast number of causes and as many treatments and responses. In any one single case, there may be several causes and several responses. There may well be spiritual elements to your pain, but that will not be the only thing.

Two. If you feel there is a spiritual aspect to your pain, rather than consider it as necessary suffering, consider what it is teaching you (if indeed it is teaching you anything – it might not be).

Three. Consider the notion that pain, rather than being spiritual in and of itself, is perhaps an obstacle to that which is spiritual. And I offer that thought with some considerable trepidation, given my concern not to have pain classed as anything especially spiritual at all.

The wise spiritual adherent will consider the spiritual implications of any pain, as they should, but be wary of adding additional unnecessary suffering from the burden of black-and-white, fundamentalist thinking about what pain is and isn't. Like everything, the truth is more than likely in the grey.

People aren't in our lives to teach us lessons (and then leave)

People come into our lives for a million different reasons, but if there's one single spiritual reason, it's this: so we can learn to love ourselves and others more. That's it. If there is one universal truth about people and their roles in our lives, it's to love each other.

A corollary to the bullshit idea that everyone we meet is there to teach us a lesson, is the notion that *the universe takes bad people out of our lives to make room for better ones.* Please: you've been reading too many memes on Facebook.

People come and go from our lives, and it's often very painful. We try to rationalise it and move on from it, with reference to a lot of spurious wisdom like *Just let it go.* Instead, be with the pain. Eventually it will go. You *will* learn from it, but that lesson is not necessarily why that person came into your life; it's at best a consequence of them leaving.

There's no such thing as an eight week total transformation

Miracle transformations rarely occur, be they your weight, your finances, or your vibration, and to invest in this possibility can be a childish folly. When you fully understand that change only occurs when you're ready to take responsibility and make it happen yourself, then there's a much better chance it will happen.

By all means, invest in learning and assistance – there's so much available – but do not give up your own power for transformation to a marketing gimmick. It will only ever be you that will make it happen.

Marketing is a science with decades of trial and error, experimentation, and expertise behind it. We are all pushovers for it every day and we are more exposed to it than we've ever been. Advertisements in the spiritual industry are no less advanced and effective than any other, and when we are desperate for change and happiness and success, and to know *exactly* why we're here and what our purpose is, then we're sensitive to promises of metamorphosis.

No truly useful and valuable teacher will make such promises, because they know that realistically your change will come incrementally and from within, and that their role is only to guide and support.

Be wary of promises of total rebirth – they're not realistic. You're likely to be fleeced, and you're setting yourself up to fail.

Karma is not going to 'get' the people you don't like

Seriously, grow the fuck up.

How often do we hear people say things like *I don't have to do anything because karma will get them?*

Karma is not punishment. For you or anyone else. Nor is it about reward. Nor is it some external force, like a God, that exacts revenge. (In fact, I think we've created karma into a type of God by thinking of it this way. It's as though we *have* to have some external power to blame – anything but take responsibility for ourselves.) Karma is also not something that is fated. It's not a spiritual spreadsheet that balances out the good and bad you do by enacting good and bad consequences.

So, to be clear:

- Karma is not punishment.
- Karma is not reward.
- Karma is not an external force.
- Karma is not fated.
- Karma is not a spiritual spreadsheet.
- Karma is not a result (or a consequence or an after affect).

The way people bandy about the word *karma* is almost a kind of cultural misappropriation. It hijacks and abuses a key concept of Buddhism.

Karma means action. It is our intentional actions, behaviours and thoughts. It's the energy we create with the emotion and vibration that accompanies our actions (and thoughts and behaviours).

If our actions are accompanied by anger and bitterness, then that is the energy that is around us and with which we will continue to feed everything else we do. If our actions are accompanied by love, then that is the energy that feeds us and our actions.

> How people treat you is their karma;
> how you react is yours.
>
> *Wayne Dyer*

Your karma is about you, and my karma is about me. You don't get to decide what my karma is or should be. It's literally none of your business.

Not Bullshit

There are seven billion ideas of what spiritual is

Among the adherents of a single religion, there are multiple views of what that religion's truth is. Even among those who would profess not to believe in anything spiritual, there are many different philosophies of life. There is no one way. Some Christians like to remind us that *Jesus is the way,* by which they mean the *only* way. I don't believe the *only way* part of it, but at any rate, Jesus' *way* was simply to take a spiritual path, to be committed to it, to adhere to human and humane principles of life and love, and to share these with people he knew. Seems a pretty good *way* to me. It's pretty much what I'm aiming for in this life. Guess that makes me a Christian. The Buddha had more or less the same idea. Guess that makes me a Buddhist too. And a Hindu and a Muslim, a Hare Krishna and a Jew. No wonder I became a Baha'i.

There are almost unlimited paths up the mountain.
If you're shouting at everyone that they're on the wrong path,
you are the one not getting to the top.

Sue Fitzmaurice

Maybe the spiritual path you're walking right now is one of forgiveness. Of yourself and others. Maybe you're facing your shame – your dark side – and integrating it lovingly back into who you are. Maybe your path right now is one of self-discipline. Maybe it's about joy. These and many other roads will help you grow and vibrate higher, and become a better you.

Every one of us is operating from our own unique view of the world, within a context of what we understand, overlaid with what we desire, overlaid with the lessons confronting us, overlaid with our unique emotional makeup, overlaid with the support and love of people around us, overlaid, overlaid, overlaid. My own path is as different from the people closest to me as it is from any one of a million people whose lives are utterly different from mine.

There is no point trying to convince anyone of a spiritual truth.
Share, but don't waste energy *convincing.*

Sue Fitzmaurice

There are thousands of religions in the world today. Most people believe in just one of them and consider all the others false. A lot of people think they're all false. And much the same can be said of what is considered non-religious, spiritual truth. (It always amuses me that fundamentalist religionists and die-hard atheists have so much in common in rejecting all, or virtually all, of the rest of humanity's beliefs.)

Say not, I have found the truth, but rather, I have found a truth.
Say not, I have found the path of the soul.
Say rather, I have met the soul walking upon my path.
For the soul walks upon all paths. The soul walks not upon a line,
neither does it grow like a reed. The soul unfolds itself like a
lotus of countless petals.

Kahlil Gibran

There's no right or wrong spiritual experience. There's no better or best way to love God. God is whatever you understand God to be.

Spirituality is dirty work

If you've created a shelter of total harmony and angels around you, then you may well have created a wall to hide you from the real work of your spiritual journey. Nothing against harmony or angels – the more the merrier, and angels *will* protect you and even signpost your journey – but beware you're not creating obstacles that obscure the truth of the spiritual journey.

Real faith has no easy answers. It involves an ongoing struggle,
a continual questioning of what we think we know.

Lesley Hazleton

Spirituality is not pretending you're always in a good mood. It's not about having a perfect and quiet life. Spirituality is dynamic – it's heaving with energy – it's about being on fire. It's about getting your face and hands dirty, making mistakes, and occasionally pissing people off, not intentionally but because you're going one way and they're going another and sometimes we bump into each other. Healing can be ugly. It's not all light and love. It's digging into your own 'stuff' and that can be scary.

The road to enlightenment is long and difficult,
and you should try not to forget snacks and magazines.

Anne Lamott

If you're pretending everything is beautiful all the time, you're not just deluding yourself, you're defrauding yourself. You're missing out on the reality of spiritual growth and development. Which can just as often be about the mud and the dust from which we fashion the bricks that then have to be fired before they can contribute to the construction of anything solid.

Substantive spirituality – real growth – is built on the back of steps of agonising progress.

Your dark you is a part of you

We all have a shadow side. It's that part of us that contains everything we never want others to see. It's our shame and our embarrassment, it's our stifled anger and our hidden rage. It's all the things we've been taught to suppress, perhaps in favour of feigned sweetness and positivity at all costs.

Find those things – the shame and embarrassment and anger – and embrace them. They are part of you, and together with all that's brilliant and dazzling about you, they make you whole. Face your shame, get to know it, show it some warmth and love, build a relationship with it so that it doesn't feel isolated and alone. It's not going to bite you. Except if you ignore it, then it will almost certainly snap at you when you're looking the other way.

If you're 'awake', then your darkness can serve your light. (If you're not awake, it's just darkness.) We don't grow our own light by ignoring our darkness; we do so by shining a light on the dark and bringing it into the light. This is truly divine work. It's hard work. It hurts, it humiliates, it can make us feel small. But pain is only healed in the light.

By accepting the inevitability of our shadow, we recognize that we are also what we are not. This humbling recognition restrains us from the madness of trying to eliminate those we hate and fear in the world. Self-mastery, maturity, and wisdom are defined by our ability to hold the tension between opposites.

Louis G. Herman

Science

There's a fairly strong anti-science bent among much of the spiritual community. Not altogether unreasonably, much of that stems from a mistrust of a medical science that hasn't always provided the right answers or the best outcomes for many. Much of it stems also from either laziness, or an inability to grasp the actual science, which is not a valid argument against it.

It's that same mistrust that rejects religion for its failings, politicians for their failings, the education system for its failings, and so on. It's the application of a set of blinkers such as these that means we continually throw the baby out with the bathwater. This lack of discernment undermines our own credibility and that of the important teachings the spiritual arena has to offer the world.

Anti-science views stem also from the frustration that many of our own esoteric beliefs fail current scientific tests of truth. I don't have a problem that much of what I believe isn't scientifically proven – I'm happy to accept (perhaps a little too conveniently) that those things just aren't proven *yet*. I don't, however, reject science in return. It was one of the attractions I had to the Baha'i Faith, that we must seek the unity of science and religion.

Science is not only compatible with spirituality; it is a profound source of spirituality. When we recognize our place in an immensity of light years and in the passage of ages, when we grasp the intricacy, beauty and subtlety of life, then that soaring feeling, that sense of elation and humility combined, is surely spiritual. The notion that science and spirituality are somehow mutually exclusive does a disservice to both.

Carl Sagan

Modern medicine is improving all the time and without doubt has contributed to our much-extended lifespan as a species. Rejecting its options out of hand, without broad consideration and a surfeit of advice, is foolhardy. We risk the same fallibility of a fundamentalist community that rejects climate change. Fortunately, most in the spiritual community accept this particular scientific reality and are even ardent proponents of climate action.

We can have a reasonable scepticism about most things but we need to be wary of our own dogma and potential for closed-mindedness. We're a tiny blue dot in the vast ocean that is the universe – there is room yet for both science and spirituality.

The first gulp from the glass of natural sciences will make you an atheist, but at the bottom of the glass God is waiting for you.

Werner Heisenberg (father of Quantum Physics)

Doing your time

It's considered a characteristic of the *Millennial* generation that they want everything now, in double-quick time, without particularly having put in a lot of effort. Life is a huge challenge for our children's generation (mine are in their twenties), much more so than it was for ours (I'm in my fifties). I don't believe the notion that they're unwilling to do their time as much as I think their world is fiercer and they feel they have to push hard to make their dreams come true. It is however a characteristic of many who've started a spiritual journey to believe they not only have all the answers but they've reached some pinnacle of spiritual wayfaring after five minutes.

Your spiritual journey is never ending. You don't ever arrive somewhere and then there's nowhere else to go. There's always more. Anyone attempting to convince you of their beliefs has forgotten this basic tenet, because if they were continuing on their journey – if they knew the truth of their journey was that it didn't end – then they would know that what they believe now is relative and therefore not the whole truth and therefore not a thing to convince others of. It's great to share your beliefs – always share when you're invited to – but it's ignorant to try to convince others of them. I'm not interested in soapboxes. I'll happily share with you if you'll share with me, but I won't listen to you preaching at me. The truths worth exploring are those put with love and without the need to dominate or to convince. Look for the soft-spoken over the zealot always.

I've spent my entire life, from early childhood on, exploring and participating in the religious and spiritual. I've done my time. My spiritual life is extremely solid. I'm more open than most, but do not come at me with your year-old wisdom, or your one Faith way. Get some time and experience and perspective up your sleeve.

If you've had a spiritual awakening, your next best step is to shut up and listen. Rather than proclaiming your new-found wisdom to the world, you may do well to hold your tongue about it for a while and continue learning, especially before you presume to start teaching. There are a million other experiences you can have, to add to your one. Try at least another dozen or two of them, across a range of traditions. Real spiritual growth is a life's journey and work, not a switch that's suddenly been turned on.

Spirituality is about seeking, not having sought. On the spiritual path, *doing your time* doesn't really end either. It's an ever-evolving quest. If you've been on a spiritual adventure for a long time, you can probably think back to a lot of things you once believed in that are no longer true for you, or that have changed. Becoming more spiritual doesn't mean becoming more fixed in our beliefs – it means becoming more open about them. It's not about becoming more certain, although it's not about becoming more uncertain especially either, but it is about certainty not being so relevant anymore. Certainty is an illusion. Certainty brings less spiritual growth.

Get real

Having a spiritual life doesn't mean rejecting what's rational. In fact, it means much more the opposite. We observe and accept reality in order to grow spiritually. I'm not talking here about the difference between the physical and spiritual worlds – of course we are learning detachment from aspects of the former and working out how to more easily locate and experience the latter. I'm talking about not pretending that everything is sweetness and light when it isn't.

I'm talking about accepting the truth of your situation – maybe that you're jobless and unwell – rather than pretending that those things don't matter because you're living a spiritual life.

I'm talking about accepting the truth of science and not making up your own science – or anti-science – because it suits your spiritual beliefs to do so.

I'm talking about if you want to be a Christian then you need to act like one.

I'm talking about if you want to be spiritual then you need to be practising love and compassion first and foremost.

I'm talking about recognising when your ego is in charge and learning to manage it.

I'm talking about not blaming others for your situation.

I'm talking about realising you might have a few unpleasant traits yourself and it's not always the other person.

I'm talking about having your eyes open, as well as your heart.

Don't bullshit yourself. Wake up to your own crap – we all have plenty of it – your spiritual path has to entail you owning it and cleaning it up.

Keep it simple

Don't make life too hard for yourself. You don't have to figure out every past life to understand every dark element of your present one. Common sense is your friend.

A simple rule: if you're happy, it's working; if you're constantly miserable, try another tack. If you're triggered by other people, look in the mirror.

Love is the answer. Of yourself and others.

Responsibility and discernment

Responsibility isn't guilt, and discernment isn't judgement. Stick with responsibility and discernment – guilt and judgement are crap and they'll make you ill. There is a million miles of difference between responsibility and guilt, if you're discerning enough to realise. See what I did there?

Discernment is a higher-order thought process. It has nothing to do with putting people and things into labelled boxes and everything to do with assisting you to refine your own path. Judgement and discernment are not only not different ends of a spectrum, they're different spectrums.

The judgement spectrum extends from one end where you might think to yourself *well, I wouldn't go out dressed like that!* through to *that person's energy is so negative* and further along the other end to *all white men are arseholes.*

The discernment spectrum goes from *I think people can dress how they want* through to *that person must be having a hard time – how can I help* and further along to *white men are the most privileged group in society.*

It's the same with guilt and responsibility. The guilt spectrum goes from *I really screwed up* to *I'm a horrible person* to *I hate myself.*

The responsibility spectrum goes from *I'll do better next time* to *Everyone doesn't have to like me* to *I love myself.*

We all fall very easily into guilt and judgement. We're so good at it that when we drop into it, we can feel really guilty about it and judge ourselves harshly. That's the insidious danger of guilt and judgement. They create never-ending spirals of harm, to ourselves and others.

Guilt and judgement arise out of fear and self-loathing. Responsibility and discernment arise out of openness and self-love. They are worlds apart but yet we flip very easily from discernment into judgement, and from responsibility into guilt. Even with decades of practice, we will still slip into them. These are the most challenging, and yet most rewarding, of spiritual lessons, and ones that we need to remind ourselves of frequently. If there's not kindness in the words and thoughts we have of ourselves and others, then we've spilled over into the dark side. When you feel yourself going there, bring some love and light into the arena, and you'll more easily move away.

Remember not to beat yourself up when you stumble. You're human. Be gentle with yourself.

The practice of discernment is a part of higher consciousness.
Discernment is not just a step up from judgement; it is the
opposite. Through judgement we reveal what we need to
confront and learn. Through discernment we reveal
what we have mastered.

Glenda Green

A good contradiction is a good thing

This is one of my favourite pieces of life wisdom, and I think one of the most important truths of all, ever. More people need to learn to cope with, and even love, contradiction. Contradiction is great. There is truth in contradiction. In fact, it's the only right way to read this book, because it's *laden* with contradiction.

Humans crave absolute certainty; they aspire to it;
they may pretend, as practitioners of certain religions do,
to have attained it. But science teaches us that the most we can
hope for is successive improvement in our understanding,
learning from our mistakes, a variable approach to the universe,
and with the proviso that absolute certainty will always elude us.

Carl Sagan

I don't respect harsh scepticism any more than I like blind faith, but healthy scepticism is a gift. It allows you to ask questions and check things out via other sources. We're overloaded with information today and we accept too much of it too easily. If you think you have all the answers, think again. Then again. It doesn't mean you to have to doubt everything – it does mean verifying information before you take it as gospel.

We like having answers. It gives us security and comfort. But it's not always where wisdom is to be found. Most real truth exists in the grey. If the truth you're proclaiming is black and white – right or wrong, do or die – then it's almost certainly lacking.

We must be fully committed, but we must also be aware at the
same time that we might possibly be wrong.
Our commitment to an idea is healthiest
when it is not without doubt, but in spite of doubt.

Rollo May

One of the realities of being committed to a degree of uncertainty, is that you'll find it difficult to find your place. Sceptics, even moderate ones, aren't welcome in a majority of religious and spiritual spheres. Curiosity and questions are rarely valued in any fundamentalist or dogmatic place, including many so-called spiritual ones.

I have approximate answers and possible beliefs
and different degrees of certainty about different things,
but I'm not absolutely sure about anything.

Richard Feynman, physicist

As any researcher will tell you, it's not about what you know, it's about *questioning* what you know.

Every time we think we have certainty about life
– whether from mathematics, logic, religion, politics or ideology
– we have lost the primary experience.
We have deformed our essential humanity
and closed down the search. Disaster looms.

Louis G. Herman

The law of attraction only works if you do

Two friends had the opportunity to submit a collection of art on a particular theme for a contest with a well-known gallery. Only one person would win the large cash prize, although several more would have the chance to show their work in the gallery. One of my friends had been painting for several years and had already sold a lot of work. She set about, with planning and focus, to produce the collection of several pieces required, knowing precisely how much time she needed – they had about six months – to produce a collection of that size, aware she would paint two or three times the number of pieces required in order to choose which went into her final submission. On several occasions she offered to assist our less experienced friend and offered advice on planning and all manner of elements necessary to producing a professional collection of this size.

Our other friend didn't start working on her collection until a few weeks before the deadline and didn't seek any help or advice from the more experienced friend. Meanwhile though, for the entire period since the contest opened, she 'held space' for the win, convinced that as long as she put enough positive thought into it, she would win, or at least have her work accepted. Ultimately the more experienced artist's work was accepted to hang in the gallery, a great affirmation of not only her skill and experience but the extent of effort she'd put into the process. The other friend was not only not successful, but was enraged at the friend who'd done the work and succeeded.

There are a few things to say about this:

1. Do the bloody work! Don't bullshit yourself that you're going to attract the ultimate prize when you have done the minimum amount possible.
2. Your ability to make the law of attraction work for you is dependent on not just doing the outer work, but also on doing the inner work. You can't skip over the part about your inner self believing you're not going to make it, or that you're not good enough, or that nothing good ever happens to you. You've got to have done that bit of work in order for 'holding space' for the win to actually have any chance of success. Forcing your mind to concentrate on the win is an act of intellectual discipline that overrides your heart and soul – it could work, but more than likely it won't. Your desire for the win has to be tied to your true heart's desire and your soul's purpose, and you have to have made space for that by doing the healing work of your heart and soul. If your desire for the win is tied up with your ego, it won't happen, because your ego is in the way.
3. If you're not prepared to accept a close friend's win as great news, then again, your ego is in the way.
4. If you can't accept that in this case the law of attraction did actually work, but for someone else, then you have missed the point of the law of attraction.

It's exhausting devoting massive amounts of energy to holding space, particularly if you find it not working every time you attempt it. It would be reasonable to lose faith in the whole notion. Part of the problem is that these complex spiritual concepts are portrayed by the spiritual community as being simple and straightforward and they're not. They take practice, and that practice has to occur within a context of gentleness with one's self, and a relative lack of attachment to outcomes.

So often we don't bother learning the deeper and more intricate aspects of these important spiritual principles. Or we go into some other self-critical mode to explain why it's not working. Other people like to 'help' us with our own self-criticism: *You must have some karma you need to work through* or *It's probably some past life trauma* or *Your crown chakra is probably blocked.* Take it easy. You can go down a metaphysical road that veers off into a thousand other back roads and alleyways that will have you going around in circles.

In the end, spirituality is not a justification for failing to take responsibility for your actions. It's easy to make the standard mantras fit a situation, and whilst there are layers of truth in the idea that the universe brings us what we need, or that we're responsible for what we attract, these can be excuses for not taking responsibility ourselves, and/or a stick with which to beat ourselves unnecessarily.

Get a sense of humour

Arguably the greatest spiritual leader in the world today is the Dalai Lama. Ever seen how much that man laughs? And he doesn't just laugh – he giggles. Like a schoolboy. And as far as I can tell, it's very often at himself.

The more we develop spiritually, the less seriously we take just about everything. Especially ourselves. Spiritual growth necessarily involves having less attachment to the material, to our thoughts, and to things that go on around us. This doesn't mean that one becomes callous and unfeeling – in fact we become more compassionate. But we begin to see the extent to which we overreact to so much that goes on in our lives, and after a while a lot of things start to look plain silly.

Laughter and joy are at the very centre of the spiritual experience, or should be.

And in my experience, any angel worth its salt is wicked funny and enjoys a good laugh.

Laughing at ourselves, loud and often, means we're no longer attached to our own and others' ideas about who and what we are. We stop being offended. This a fantastic place to reach.

If you're easily offended, or unable to laugh at yourself, you've probably got a humour deficit. Blow the budget on this one and get back in the black – you'll go a long way.

The truth about ego

This is the hub of a lot that goes wrong with spirituality and religion. If the expression of your spirituality and your spiritual beliefs includes displays of hostility, self-importance and intolerance, then it's not spirituality you're practising. If you're uncomfortable around someone you judge to be of a lesser consciousness than you, that's not spirituality, that's ego. Nor is it about them, it's about you. If your spirituality was where you think it is, you'd be fine around any level of consciousness. Spirituality is not a decoration for your ego.

The reality of course is that many people make us feel uncomfortable, for a whole raft of reasons. If someone is a physical threat, get the hell out of there. If you're in a relationship with a horrific narcissist who's lying to you and cheating on you, probably get the hell out of there.

If you're feeling uncomfortable because of someone's 'energy' though, look to yourself, because it's almost certainly not about the other person.

This isn't about denying your own truth; it's about being comfortable enough with your own truth that you can be with people who don't share it. You may have meditated till the cows come home but if you can't treat other people with respect, it's meaningless.

Having said that, the people I've come a cropper with more than any other are those who share more or less the identical beliefs to me, and they've still beaten me up with their spiritual cudgels. I've occasionally realised too late that some people are not the open and warm people I thought they were. They were cold, with an airbrush of glitter.

Everyone is on a spiritual path, even if they don't realise it. If in any way we want to assist others on their path, our primary tool is love. Or at the very least to be nice.

If we're not able to do that, then ego is in the way and it needs confronting. And what precisely needs confronting will be different for all of us. It's just another part of our own dark side. We all have one, and we need to get to know it, care for it, bring it into the light and integrate it into who we are. The reactions we have to other people are a tool for identifying elements of our own darkness, not for whipping those other people.

Cussing with joy

I find swearing a great joy. I neither consider it spiritual nor unspiritual. I'm not interested in shocking the old and set-in-their-ways however, so I'll refine my language around some, but if you're not old and infirm I'm not going out of my way for you.

Making someone's language – or the way they dress, or what they eat – a measure of their spirituality is bullshit. I could say it's fucking bullshit, but I won't. Oops.

See *Judging others.*

I'm an expert only in myself; and even then, not so much

The first thing you should know about me is that I am not you. A lot more will make sense after that.

Unknown

I'm an expert on me; hopefully it goes without saying therefore that you are *not* an expert on me. You probably don't know me, but if by chance you do, unless you've really engaged with me about the depths of who I am in the last couple of years – or frankly the last six months – then you don't know me. I'm a very different person from the one I was two years ago. I'm different from the person I was six months ago. I intend to be different again in another six months. I'm still figuring myself out, and I know you're still figuring yourself out too. I'm barely an expert in myself, so I won't presume to be one on you.

Pronouncing on other people's character is the most damaging, unkind, and least spiritual thing you can do for them. And if you consider yourself spiritual and that person is a friend of yours, then you really need to take a look at yourself, because you're way off track.

Beyond Bullshit

Spirituality is confusing. We get lost, we get found, we get lost again. Our heart, our mind and our soul give us different messages at different times and at different levels of awareness, sometimes – often – contradicting each other. It can be hard to know what is true, and which truth is the higher one.

We can all feel the need to proclaim our truth, not least in order to understand it better ourselves; as well as to be able to identify who we are. Our identities are important to us. Knowing who we are contributes to our self-esteem and gives us confidence. But the extent to which we proclaim it can serve to isolate others, and thus in turn ourselves. When our work is in the spiritual arena, then we can be even more intent on identifying our beliefs and what we stand for and thus we run the risk of being even more segregating.

Language is important. The words we use and how we use them make a difference in the lives of everyone who hears them.

Discernment, and reducing black-and-white thinking, are massively important. Cause and effect aren't always the same in every instance, and rarely are things always one way or the other. Most of life happens in the grey.

Life is complex and we want to be able to simplify by putting things easily into boxes and categories: eg. *It's all a gift from the universe.* No. It's not. You made some of that happen yourself, the good and the bad.

In the end, love is what matters most. Love yourself, and love whoever else is around to be loved.

Moving beyond confusion

Faced with endless possibilities for spiritual knowledge and understanding, and combined with the judgements and verdicts of many of one's fellow spiritual journeyers, it's easy to feel lost. When we're searching for answers, we can quickly grab hold of one particular set of beliefs and cling on for dear life. In a world of increasing uncertainty, it feels safe and secure.

Real spiritual growth is never ending, and the best gems are often found at the bottom of wells of challenge and confusion. Get a few good friends around you who won't let you drown, and head down those wells.

To the extent that you're prepared to live with lack of clarity, at least from time to time, you will find when you do come upon clarity again, all shiny and pretty, it's likely to be more solid and true than before. Until the next well comes along for you to plumb.

Confusion, as with truth, is relative. If you're in it, remember the many truths you've already found that continue to serve you well. Things will become clear. Don't be despondent. In my experience, confusion is a herald for clarity. The more we simply allow the confusion, the sooner it passes. It's a relationship between you and the universe – as you continue to seek, it continues to reveal. But sometimes in order to see what is revealed, you necessarily have to acquire more spiritual vision, and that process inherently creates confusion, as we give up and let go and brave the unknown.

Heart and soul

Spirituality necessarily has to focus on the expansion of your heart and soul. These are the places in you that you need to need to try to operate from.

It's from our heart and soul that our happiness and growth spring from. If you're operating in love and joy – the true expressions of our heart and soul – you'll attract more of the same. Correspondingly, if you're operating in fear and shame, you'll attract more of that.

When in doubt, locate your heart. If the truth – or a truth – is unclear, locate the spirit within you and commune with it. If what you feel and hear within you is angry or bitter or ashamed or judging of yourself or others, then keep looking because you haven't found it yet. It's there, but you've got some bullshit in the way.

Ego

Your ego is not something you should feel you need to destroy or even control particularly. It's a part of us we need to locate, get to know, and make friends with. It has an important role in protecting us, although it can be way too risk averse at times and prevent us from growing.

Learn to differentiate between your ego and reality. Develop your awareness of the plethora of fake news going on in your own mind. That's ego. Don't allow it to set the agenda. Introduce it to your heart and soul. Get clear on which one is which and allow your heart and soul to enfold and protect your ego, but without allowing its bullshit to block them.

When you understand that other people's behaviour is to do with how they feel about themselves; when you take responsibility for your own emotions and stop blaming others; when you stop allowing bitterness to control your thoughts and actions; then you're getting a handle on your ego.

Spiritual gaslighting

Gaslighting is manipulating someone into doubting their own sanity. It's an utterly dehumanising thing to do. Spiritual gaslighting is doing a similar thing, via the propagation of spiritual bullshit, to make someone doubt their worth as a human being. It's soul destroying and it's one of the most shite things you can do to another person. Fucking stop it. You don't get to decide someone else's spirituality. You get to love them – that's your primary job when it comes to assisting anyone on their spiritual path.

Of course you can talk with someone about whether perhaps their beliefs are harming them or others, but you don't get to convince someone they're crazy by expounding on where you think their energy is at or on the truth of their spiritual experiences.

Allowing

In order to protect our spiritual bubbles, we very easily run away from people and things that make us feel uncomfortable. If you're committed to your spiritual journey, then this is truly where you need to enlighten the fuck up. Sit with what challenges you. This is a fundamental part of the spiritual journey. If you constantly walk away from what triggers you, then you're walking away from the greater discovery of your own heart and soul and the furtherance of your spiritual path. And when you do that you're just going to add to your suffering in the long run, not diminish it.

This is non-resistance, and for all the sense of softness that that term conjures up, it's really, really hard. It involves patience and love and constant deference to our heart and soul. It's normal to want to avoid suffering, but refusing to examine our pain takes us away from our spiritual path.

The opposite of resistance is allowing. Allowing is a very feminine characteristic. It recognises that we grow and heal incrementally and with love. Allowing undermines the poison of judging – it lets things *be*. It recognises that we have all done harm and that our shame will slip away when we stop battling it.

Be prepared to toss out all that you know and believe

For those of us pursuing a religious and/or spiritual path, our beliefs form a part of our identity. Sometimes they're almost our entire identity. Eventually, all our beliefs become obstacles though. Anything we hold on to tightly enough will limit us.

If I said to you, *tomorrow you're going to wake up and everything you believe is going to be presented to you, indisputably, as a lie,* how would you feel? Would you wonder who on Earth you were without those beliefs? Because if you don't know who you are without your beliefs then you've lost the spiritual path.

You will find – if you haven't already – that once you start treating your ego with respect, that it doesn't necessarily reciprocate. It doesn't mean to, but it gets very sneaky. One of the things it likes to do is create in you an unwitting attachment to your beliefs. In this way it controls your spiritual path, steering you away from potential pain and suffering, which is, after all, its job. You end up getting stuck in a spiritual groove – you're like a fish with a three-second memory, swimming round the same small bowl going *Ooh, isn't this pretty! Ooh, isn't this pretty! Ooh, isn't this pretty!* Do ya'self a favour.

You might believe you're the incarnation of Isis, but if you're not dealing with your shit, it's a meaningless belief.

More to the point though, the spiritual realm is vast. Any one of us can conceive of only the tiniest part of it in any one moment. Why would you not want to discover more than just the one wee piece you've experienced thus far?

Stop overreacting

A large percentage of our reactions to events around us, and others' behaviours, involve more emotion than they deserve. And we generally think we're entitled to our reactions. With perhaps a few exceptions, to the extent that those reactions are inflicted on others, we're not in the least bit entitled to them.

If you've chosen a spiritual path, your responsibility is to own your own reactions, examine them, consider why they are what they are, and work out what it is that lies beneath them that needs working on.

Instead, our tendency is to not only maintain our reaction, but to look around for other things we can apply to a situation or a person to bolster our original reaction. We're especially good at this when we first realise that we've over-reacted. We'll add things to it to justify it, and before you know it, we've utterly crucified someone who might have quite unconsciously slighted us in the most insignificant of ways.

Don't be this kind of nob. Humble pie actually tastes better than you think – well, in the long run anyway. If you've over-reacted, own it. Apologise. Deal with your shit. And then next time round, as a friend of mine recently said, *Put your vehicle in neutral!*

Stop talking bullshit

There are depths and nuances to all spiritual truths – stop proclaiming superficial versions of them – you're just fucking yourself and others up. And besides, the really gorgeous growth and experience is deeper, in the nuance, in the delicate bliss of understanding that springs from connecting to the truth with your heart and soul.

If you're working in the spiritual arena, you must make a greater effort to take your understanding, and your ability to put things into words, to a greater level of intricacy. Do not communicate complex, multi-level spiritual concepts as trite social media memes unless and until you've grasped them from their multiple angles. Learn to communicate better. Stop with the frivolous and one-dimensional. If you want to take people on a spiritual journey, don't sell quick fixes and witless, half-baked concepts. If you do, you're dumbing people down and screwing them up.

Spirituality is not a race

No one is ahead of you or behind you. You're not more or less enlightened. No one else can be on your path and you can't walk someone else's. We're all journeying at our own pace.

Growth doesn't happen in a straight line either. You don't start *here* and get to *there*. You start where you are, and you walk whatever windy path you're guided along. Almost by definition, there is no such thing as a diversion – it's all grist for the mill.

And if there are any rules at all, I believe they are simply these: to learn to love yourself and others more.

We have all hurt someone tremendously, whether by intent or accident. We have all loved someone tremendously, whether by intent or accident. It is an intrinsic human trait, and a deep responsibility, to be an organ and a blade. But learning to forgive ourselves and others because we have not acted wisely is what makes us most human. We make horrible mistakes. It's how we learn. We breathe love. It's how we learn. And it is inevitable.

Nayyira Waheed

Acknowledgements

Thanks to Detta Darnell, Michelle Gould, Marg Pinsent, and especially Jo Beth Young and Helen Ross, for their contributions to the list.

I'm very grateful to Doreen Devoy Hulgan, Swati Nigam, Michelle and Marg, and all the members of the *Spiritual Bullshit* feedback group for their very useful comments and many suggested edits.

Massive thanks to Brenda Kübler for applying her brilliant editing software and picking up every one of my many inconsistencies and challenging me on my several personal punctuation 'rules' that no one else in the world has.

Special thanks to Narissa Tuawhiorangi for creating the graphic of the confused monk on the cover. Narissa also designed the final Rebel Magic Books logo.

Claire Findlater is a constant no-bullshit advisor, and brilliant wordsmith, editor, creative consultant and friend. The idea of a Zorro-masked white rabbit for the Rebel Magic Books logo was also hers.

The last couple of years have been a massive period of spiritual growth for me, which also by necessity means that a lot of it was really difficult. I've been lucky to have the support of some powerful and loving women. I hope you all know who you are because I hope I've told you enough how grateful I am that you helped me keep my head above water.

About the Author

Sue Fitzmaurice is a New Zealander, currently travelling the world. She has spent most of her working life in business, for herself and others. Sue has degrees in political science, international relations, and business. She has two adult children.

www.rebelmagicbooks.com

Made in the USA
Monee, IL
01 July 2022